T0365279

ONLY GOD CAN
TURN THIS MESS INTO HIS
MESSAGES

LUCIA ST MONICA

WESTBOW
PRESS®
A DIVISION OF THOMAS NELSON
& ZONDERVAN

WestBow Press books may be ordered through booksellers or by contacting:

WestBow Press
A Division of Thomas Nelson & Zondervan
1663 Liberty Drive
Bloomington, IN 47403
www.westbowpress.com
844-714-3454

ISBN: 978-1-6642-9197-3 (sc)
ISBN: 978-1-6642-9198-0 (hc)
ISBN: 978-1-6642-9196-6 (e)

Library of Congress Control Number: 2023902662

Print information available on the last page.

WestBow Press rev. date: 04/18/2023

For my son.
The sky is not your limit. It's just a stepping-stone.

Our life's story does not exist. There are too many seasons to put onto one such label, yet they continuously smear across a canvas creating a work of art—however changeable to the point of view.

CONTENTS

Part III
Untitled

Part IV
The Light in the Darkness

Part V
The Mercurial Debacle Resurfaced

Part VI
The Fiat End

Part VII
Tabula Rasa

Part VIII
It Is Well with My Soul

Part IX
Evolution

THE PRUNING

They stomped their feet with a hammering force as if trying to break through the bleachers. Shouting with exalting enthusiasm, the Aqua Net nest of Chrissy Thompson back flipped across the auditorium floor to the speed of pounding drums. Her bouquet of pom-poms were tossed up like fireworks, and they caught the skirt in a grasp that seemed impossible to survive. The bottom row rose first to their feet, and then their arms flowed overhead one at a time up and then down like the wave of a bed sheet thrusting into the air. Trumpets blew, and jocks charged the glossy hardwood, screaming fiercely and aimlessly as if they were looking for the win they had just won. The ambience overflowed with deafening excitement to welcome the end of senior year, and a shiny, promising future was up for grabs. I sat motionless on the right side in the top row. My head spun, and I was suddenly engulfed by an empty pit of an unknown future.

At seventeen, life seemed long.

And then, thirty years had gotten behind me. I had been abruptly plucked from the safety of serenity as if my life were a flower held by a giant who pulled off the chapters of my dying petals and let them fall one by one onto vacant ground.

Like a mouse in a cage, I ran and ran to try to catch up with time only to find the stressful rush of my days forcing the sands of seconds through faster. A life that once seemed never-ending was being forfeited, and I never even bothered to jump off the spinning wheel to run in a different direction. The moment enveloped my being, and I was suddenly sitting back on the top of those high school bleachers.

As if continuing to fall through a broken time capsule, my future showed a much older corpse, barely warm, lying still on its deathbed, and my soul was restless with regret. The colorful path between faded to a tiny lost black dot as I tried to hang on in desperation with the promise of tomorrow gone. I wept for the lost opportunities of the fruitless reflection that stared back at me.

My whole life was spent waiting for someone or something to show me the way when all the while the Way was right in front of me.

Each phase played in motions that continued to flow uncontrollably until dizziness transformed itself into a tornado that finally burst from fatalism.

Somewhere along my recent and seemingly endless fields of adversities, the evolution of my spiritual maturity enlightened my mindset and transcended my thoughts, and I realized that these things didn't happen to me. They happened for me. I take no sense of gladness whatsoever over the losses in my story. As brutally heartbreaking as they are, I feel their lessons are my responsibility and privilege to share with you.

PART I

FLOWERS FOR MY HEART

With tender words, and a gentle touch that says so much. This is how I've heard that love should always be. With love light in his eyes, he'll look at me and in one bright moment, I will see that all my dreams of love are just as love should be.

—Chris Botti

PART I

FLOWERS FOR MY HEART

CHAPTER 1

A spark emerged that I never knew existed when his hand brushed against mine; we were moving in slow motion in an old-time romantic movie. My surroundings faded to a haze of meaningless nothing, and all I saw was that smile—brilliantly sweet, humble, and gentle, perfectly contoured and placed on a face of a dream that put my soul in paradise. How could a smile do all that?

I froze entranced by his presence. As if being tugged by a puppet string, my hand extended unknowingly to give him the delivery receipt. He thanked me and then left our building leaving me standing still and breathless. I was twenty-four, so blame it on my youth if you must, but even then, I didn't believe in love at first sight. In fact, I barely believed in love at all. Yet nothing like that had ever happened to me before.

"Drew. That's his name in case you're wondering. Hello?" A hand waved vigorously in front of my face. "Nora, snap out of it!" Benny said with a laugh.

I shook my head and playfully whacked his arm.

As Benny's knee came up to a side twist, he continued to tease me. "What's up with you, girl? You're looking all in love with our new water delivery guy. *Ooo—wee!* Look at you! I need to get a fire hose and cool you off."

I stomped away feeling annoyed, yet fifteen steps down the

corridor, I still heard Benny laughing and clapping. "I'm one up on you now, girl! *Ooo—wee! Ha ha!*"

I closed the door behind me and put my back against it. A copy of the receipt I was holding read Sterling Rock Water Company. *I'm still holding something that dreamy guy touched*, I thought. I pressed the paper to my heart, leaned my head back, and looked up to the heavens. Throughout the rest of the week, I was amazed by the amount of space Drew took up in my mind. I'd never known someone that beautiful could be real.

The following Monday, as he approached for his weekly delivery, I ran to the back office and hid. That was as ridiculous as if I were a thirteen-year-old schoolgirl and he was some 1980s rock star who had come to carry me away to his royal rock star palace. Since when did I start believing in fairy tales? *Get a grip,* I thought. I knew that hiding was no way to get his attention, but I was very shy about him, even more so than I usually was with someone I'd just met. To put it more accurately, I was petrified.

Every week, I waited in anticipation to see Drew again only to run away and peer over a three-quarter divider wall that separated the cubicles from the front room. I had yet to say more than two words to him, but my fantasies had been spreading like wildfire.

A month later, Benny finally agreed to at least ask Drew if he was married.

"What did Drew say?" I asked Benny.

"Oh, it totally slipped my mind to ask. My bad," Benny replied as he ran his hands down the front of his shirt and grinned with slight embarrassment. "You gotta relax, girl. He's gonna think you're too easy if you don't learn to play the game right."

A flush of annoyance ignited my feet into a forward march. Refusing to suffer through another second of unanswered questions, I made a bold dash out the showroom's front doors and caught up with Drew in the parking lot just as he was about to get into his company van. He turned around and smiled. A rush came over me, and my palms began to sweat.

"I've been wondering where you were. I haven't seen you since my first delivery," Drew said.

"Office work has kept me hidden away I guess," I replied and shrugged shyly, but fireworks exploded inside me at the thought of his wondering about me too. "We're having our annual company party, and my boss, Frank, asked me to invite you. It's this Saturday, and you can bring your wife or girlfriend."

Drew's face lit up. "That sounds fun. Is it local?"

"Yeah, it's at the Venetian Gold on Main," I said with a smile.

"Yes, I know where that is. I'm actually helping my sister this Saturday, but I'd love to stop by afterward."

"Sounds great. I'll let Frank know. My name's Nora by the way. Entertainment starts at five."

"I look forward to it," he said with his adorable smile.

"Me too," I said and I smiled back. Returning inside, I speed-walked straight past a customer, past the stained glass that displayed our company name—Trendy Art Glass and More—and shut the door behind me. I leaned my back against it again, slid down partway, and smiled in satisfaction. In five days, I would be able to spend an evening with Drew Greyson.

When Saturday finally arrived, I slipped a fitted, sparkling red dress over my light porcelain skin and put on tall, black, satin heels to heighten my five-four petite frame. My makeup was meticulously applied, and my long chestnut curls were styled back to showcase my dark-brown, almond-shaped eyes that flaunted a slightly exotic look for this special occasion. Just in case Drew was single, I wanted to look my best.

Holiday music played in the background as I worked the raffle station to promote our new product line when I noticed Drew walking through the archway of the hall. He arrived clean cut as always with the physique of a soldier dressed in a dark-gray sports jacket and a white button-down shirt with the top button unbuttoned. And he was *alone*. He approached with a certain kind of easygoing charm that made him only more desirable. The excitement of the holiday season captured the atmosphere as he stayed by my side and assisted with handing out prizes while the wait staff walked around with trays of festive hors d'oeuvres.

After the final winner was called, Drew joined Benny, Frank, and me along with two of our sales reps at our dinner table. He pulled out my chair and portrayed himself as a complete gentleman as our waiter poured from a carafe a special wine. The entrées were a fabulous choice of delicately prepared chicken parmesan with penne pasta, broiled cod in chive butter sauce with a side of wild mushroom rice, or seared beef and pepper strips over spring scallions served with double-baked potatoes. Each table had a family-size platter of sautéed mixed green beans in garlic olive oil and sea salt, fresh, warm dinner rolls, and a family-size bowl of Caesar salad. Conversations flowed easily as the dessert followed with a variety of pies including pecan, chocolate, banana cream, and rhubarb complemented by Italian cookies and gourmet coffees and teas.

As the evening was coming to a close, Drew asked if he could walk me to my car, and I agreed to that. Standing outside in the cold parking lot, he smiled. I smiled, and as time stood still before us again, I knew that someday I would marry Drew Greyson as eccentric as that may sound especially to me.

"I'm so glad you invited me tonight. There is something about you that makes me feel like I've known you my whole life," Drew said sweetly.

"Yes, it's amazing how comfortable I feel with you too." My spine tingled.

We exchanged phone numbers, and he called me that same evening. We talked until the early hours of the following morning sharing our every thought as we embraced the surreal sense of belonging.

The following day, we had our first date. Twenty years later, Drew and I had been apart only twice—heart-wrenching moments that shook me out of a content state into the rawness of hidden truth and left me blindsided and breathless.

Leaving me dead for God.

CHAPTER 2

New York City truly never sleeps, not even at 4:00 a.m. Drew and I sat in the dark in anticipation of the beginning of the parade. I was the front driver, and Drew was navigating through the direction of the wind as a balloon handler. The only way to enter this parade was to be part of a notably talented extracurricular team, a beauty queen, someone famous, or being associated with a company. We somehow barely met these guidelines as the company I worked for advertised for the parade as a perk for purchasing our products. This experience, a once-in-a-lifetime opportunity, was unfolding with a thrill as the sun slowly appeared and little, happy faces with rosy cheeks holding candies and caramel popcorn lined the streets with their families.

It was Thanksgiving 2001 when Drew invited me to his place for an entire Thanksgiving meal even though it was just the two of us. When I arrived at his apartment, the aroma enticed me from outside his front door. He had prepared everything from the turkey to the green beans, mashed potatoes, and stuffing. I brought a dessert of homemade chocolate truffles. It was a delightful first date, and I was already becoming very attracted to not only Drew's mesmerizing good looks but also to his willingness to cook and clean—every woman's dream come true.

Afterward, we watched a movie, and he asked my permission

to snuggle. Considering his size—six-two—I felt I was cuddling a gentle giant teddy bear but a naturally good, sweet, and secure one.

Almost daily, Drew began meeting me during lunch breaks sometimes with flowers but always with a warm smile, and we would walk together and talk about our day. It was flattering to feel the innocent envy of other girls in the office as they noticed the way Drew dedicated himself to me. He called me on all his breaks from work just to ask me how my day was going and to tell me he was looking forward to talking to me more in the evening. I felt desired in a way that I had never experienced before, and I started to feel hopeful that true love not only actually existed but that also I was somehow lucky enough to have it in my life. I began to imagine magical days spent with Drew.

We started seeing each other every evening and every weekend. Everything on the outside looked and felt so right, but on the inside, I sensed something about Drew that was unsettling. I couldn't put my finger on it, nor did I want to believe it. Soon after, I discovered he had pretentiously lied about owning his own business before we'd met.

"I don't know. Maybe it's no big deal," I said as I handed Benny a coffee.

Benny looked at me intensely and raised an eyebrow. "I'm sure this lie was told just to impress you. Drew obviously wants to look like he had an exciting life before he met you. This may seem innocent, but if he can lie small, he can lie big."

Even though my mind told me this lie was a red flag, my heart wanted to keep moving forward with our relationship. I took Benny's advice with a grain of salt because there were indeed too many desirable things about Drew and I'd been swept away to cloud nine since the first time I saw him. Right or wrong, there was no way I was ready to give up that feeling. Besides, it was just a little lie.

CHAPTER 3

Mistakes form when we allow ourselves to be blind
from the truth. Not because the truth can't be seen,
but because of the hope we must give up to see it.
—Nora Greyson's journal

After dating for a year, Drew and I made our first home together in a duplex apartment toward the better side of the city. He continued to indulge in the art of cooking, and we shared dinners every evening regardless of our work shifts. Embracing our new lives, sometimes, we would go out on the town or take off for a spontaneous weekend getaway sharing every smile heart to heart and hand in hand. Although we experienced the typical compromise and adjustment process of getting used to living together, we remained in harmony and in love spending every free moment together dancing slowly to the music in our kitchen. Drew always wanted to be right by my side both in and outside our home. In the beginning, there were times that felt a little suffocating, but as I became used to it, I was glad to have someone longing for my attention as much as he did. And then I started to depend on it.

During one of our mini vacations, we spoke about our future, and I shared my dream to return to college to pursue a degree in graphic design. Drew said he had an interest in becoming an electrician. Within a few months, we had signed up for school and started working toward our goals.

Two Years Later

The sun was strong on a Saturday afternoon as we frolicked through the mist of the falls. Suddenly, Drew stopped and gently grabbed my hand. He spun me around with a serious look and got down on one knee. He looked up at me and asked if I could see the tiny water bugs swimming in the puddle I was standing in barefooted. When I bent down to look, he chuckled and pulled a small jewelry box out of his pocket. He flipped it open to display a brilliant princess cut diamond set in gold. "Nora, will you marry me?" Drew asked humbly.

"Yes!" I replied with overwhelming excitement as I grabbed for the box almost knocking it into the falls. Grasping it tightly, my hand on the box, Drew's hand on mine, our hearts beating heavily while our eyes returned to each other with a sigh of relief. We gazed deeply and lovingly at one another for a moment that felt like a lifetime.

He slowly reopened the box and removed the ring to slide it onto my left ring finger—the only finger that has a vein flowing directly to the heart theoretically speaking. I swung my arms around his neck and squeezed tightly. He squeezed back and lifted me off my feet into a gentle but strong embrace, and we buried our faces in each other's necks drowning in a moment of joie de vivre. With all aspects falling into place and our hearts continuously melting together, the promises of an auspicious future had opened its doors to welcome our arrival.

Before we fell asleep that night, I whispered to Drew, "It's just you and me."

Drew replied, "You and me, forever and ever, amen."

CHAPTER 4

"As we gather here today at this joyful union before God, we promise from this day forward ..."

My white gown was draped with delicate silver threads and tiny crystal beads at its sweetheart neckline and then followed down the center back train blooming with beauty as it flowed past my clear-top silver heels, which stood at the church's altar and rested facing our guests as we exchanged vows.

I looked knowingly into Drew's deep-set, dark-blue eyes as he gazed and smiled at me. His light-blond hair was carefully groomed, and his satin lined suit made of wool and cashmere highlighted his masculine frame. He gently and securely took my hand. He was stunning.

"I will stand before you as your protector, I will stand behind you as your solace, and I will stand beside you as your peace of mind and strength in your soul. I will lie in your arms with contentment forever.

"As God's seals these words with His love, the wings of heaven wrap around our souls and bind them into one. Our love is strong as death; no flood can quench, no sorrows drown. The flame of this passion will be the flame that guides our life, through all of good times, and any of bad, until one's last breath is gone."

Hundreds of bright yellow daffodils cascaded across the cool early spring grounds below the enchanting gothic architecture of the Royal Bellezza Banquet. Bubbles drifted from mini trinkets that our guests blew from upon our arrival. Inside, the crowd was growing with excitement.

"I now announce for the first time ever *Mr. and Mrs. Andreww Greysooon*" fervently declared DJ Jax, who was dressed in black and was enthusiastically ebullient as we strutted proudly onto the dance floor hand in hand.

We danced closely to our favorite songs while being adored by our loved ones, who were enjoying the opened bar along with hors d'oeuvres of jumbo shrimp cocktail, beef tenderloin crostini, chicken and cheddar puffs, bacon-wrapped scallops, and an exotic seasonal cheese and fruit table.

Photographers snapped shots while the roaring flames in huge fireplaces illuminated the backdrop as the hosts presented our dinner plates. Prime rib, chicken cordon bleu, and sea bass with a pyramid of seafood artistically displayed on top were the choices we had for entrees—too difficult a choice. Drew and I ordered all three meals to share with each other.

Love was spread as toasts were made and utensils were tapped against wine glasses as requests for us to kiss. Most of our family was there except for Raymond, and smiles with joyful gestures lined the faces of all our guests.

As the evening was starting to close, the final course of a delightful Venetian table loaded with exquisite Italian pastries was displayed along with our wedding cake, which held combination layers of heavenly rich chocolate, fine French vanilla with chocolate mousse filling, and raspberry toppings with dark chocolate shavings.

Outside the heavy solid gate doors, we boarded a small boat and a gondolier rowed us through candle lit waters where a quiet bed and breakfast waited for our arrival. The next morning, we woke to the smell of fresh-cut flowers and a tray of warm bagels with fruit cocktail and then relaxing massages before hurrying off to catch our flight.

Our honeymoon in Aruba sizzled with a boisterous nightlife. We strolled through the streets of a Dutch colonial village and relaxed on finely groomed, sun-kissed beaches surrounded by crystal-clear oceans and quaint, colorful tiki huts with thatched roofs. We took a canoe ride on heavenly blue waters, ate conch with our hands, and enjoyed all the exotic features and romance our voyage offered.

The sunsets were stunning—the excitement was plentiful, and most of all, the passion in our room was never-ending.

CHAPTER 5

The honeymoon was a branch to our new lives as we returned to our studies and work. I graduated from graphic design school and landed my first job at a small studio on the outskirts of town. I was ecstatic over my new career and enjoyed going to work every day.

Leaving the city, we purchased our first home a few towns over. It was a small, three- bedroom ranch on a half-acre of land outlined by hydro fields under a secluded walking trail that was propped up by boards and rocks. It wasn't much of a house, but with hard work and diligence, Drew and I would transform it into a great little home.

As we stood hand in hand staring at the front with the sound of new keys looped around Drew's finger, I became overwhelmed with gratification for a rekindled nostalgia that was once tossed away so long ago, and I related a moment like this only to a pot of gold floating unreachably high up in the sky.

During our seventh year of marriage, we were delighted by the exciting news of our coming baby. The more reality settled in, the more Drew and I beamed rapturously over becoming parents and would frequently visit toy stores to amuse ourselves with all the latest baby gadgets and get lost in the wonder and joy that lay ahead.

CHAPTER 6

All is new in every type of season, blooming with delight and splendid beauty.

—Nora Greyson's journal

"There was a hole in the center of the earth. It was a very big hole, just waiting for you. And in this hole was a very big star, and this star was waiting for you. And in this star was a very bright light, and this light was waiting for you. And then one day, this very wise boy, he took this light and sprinkled it around. And around and around—and around and around—and around he went, for the whole world to see." I sang a lullaby as I gently pressed my fingertip against a single freckle on the tiny nose of this new life.

Little seven pound and five ounce Toby Elliot Greyson was born in April 2010. It was for us the truest and purest form of love swaddled with a ribbon on top of his blue hospital cap that kept his tiny head warm. Ten little fingers, ten little toes, and all smiles—you wouldn't believe how much baby Toby smiled. It was as if his old soul had knowingly emerged from the twilight of blissful sweetness where only gumdrops fell from the sky.

I returned to work after the typical three-month new-mother leave and was welcomed home each evening by Drew's loving arms.

Our house was always tidy, and our Toby was well cared for and always displaying his never-ending happiness and curiosity for life.

But financially, we faced struggles and setbacks being new parents with young careers no matter how frugal we were. Regardless, we refused to allow the lack of money to steal our joy, and so we remained in love, the three of us. Drew and I were the bread while tiny, smiling Toby was the cheese in the middle cuddling close at nighttime, cooing and reading baby books together—such a sweet, sweet life.

Drew woke up earliest each morning. Quietly, he would kiss Toby and gently smooth back the auburn fuzz on his head before changing him, and then he would lay Toby down next to me. Drew returned home before me in the evenings and gladly continued to prepare dinners on most nights. We both shared life's responsibilities—caring for Toby, splitting the shopping and the upkeep of our home. As our income improved, our lives developed a good rhythm.

As the years passed, Drew never once left for work in the morning without leaning over me while I was still sleepy in bed to hug and kiss me goodbye.

"I love you, Nora. Have a great day. I'll call you on my break," Drew would softly whisper in the dark and then do the same for Toby, who by then was walking and talking.

With the sun barely showing from the morning sky, Drew would stand for a moment in our driveway to spot Toby watching from his bedroom window, and he would wave and blow kisses before getting in his car. Filling Toby's heart with warmth, Toby would delightfully reciprocate with affection.

Drew continued to frequently call and send text messages throughout his days while we were apart during working hours just to tell me how much he loved me and missed me. We remained inseparable, and we cherished every moment as a family with our sweet, growing, energetic son. Before falling asleep at night, I still whispered, "It's just you and me," and Drew would finish the thought—"You and me, forever and ever, amen."

I felt I was living a dream, and I thanked God every day for this beautiful life.

PART II

THE CHARLATAN'S COVERT CAME UNDONE

The drunken state of a dark hidden diary will transform into the mindset of a madman, regardless the length of time successfully kept closed.
                                    —Nora Greyson's journal

CHAPTER 7

August 2015

Falene arrived with sirloin steaks for the grill, jumbo shrimp cocktail, and a summer fruit salad of fresh melons and berries. She brought squirt guns and water balloons for the kids and carried in a large gift bag for Drew. Her long, black hair was almost as bouncy as her ever-changing moods, but when she was cheerful, her face flushed like the desert sun.

Falene was Raymond's Brazilian wife, his fifth since Drew's mother, Ruby, had died, but also his longest. She was younger than Raymond by twelve years and wore it like a "You owe me" badge of honor. Holding her hairless cat, she stroked his rhinestone collar. "Hurry up, Raymond! The party isn't going to wait for you. And make sure you don't overeat while we're here."

Raymond stepped out from his fancy sports car with his too-tight golf clothes and cane. He wore his skin thick over his pointy face and gin and tonic. We hadn't seen him in about three years, but if you'd have asked Drew, he'd have told you that he hadn't seen him since he was five. That's when his mother had died.

Amie was Drew's beauty queen twin sister, both of them spitting images of their mother Ruby. Amie always had a fashion statement to announce, and that day, she wore her short, bleach- blond hair bad-to-the-bone straight and tucked behind dangling silver hoop earrings that almost brushed the shoulder of her fitted red tank top. She bubbled out of her car, and Seth, her boyfriend, in his shades and goatee followed carrying a tray of cheese and crackers and their famous stuffed mushrooms. As they approached us, Amie cast the smile of a princess.

Falene's daughter Mia ran past and jumped up to slap the bottom leaves on the tree that overhung our patio as she called out for Toby to play. The sun was so brilliant and the sky so blue one wouldn't mind relying on the balminess of the weather to forget that life could possibly hold a single sorrow. It was a perfect day to celebrate Drew's and Amie's fortieth birthdays.

Embracing Falene, Drew accidently bumped her arm and almost spilled the tray of food she was holding. I quickly caught the tray and apologized for his clumsiness. Raymond rushed to her side and soothed her hair from her forehead in an awkward fatherly way searching her face for any trace of disapproval that Drew might have caused.

Amie and I gathered easily and talked about our summer plans as the school year had just come to an end. Mia would be going off to camp, and Drew and I were planning to take Toby to the shoreline pier for their annual kid's festival. We all talked about getting together for a few day trips at some amusement parks, museums, and beaches.

The glare of the sun behind a brightly colored bouquet of balloons erased the expression on Drew's face.

"Can you give me a hand carrying some food outside?" I asked him but didn't receive an answer.

"I'll help," Amie said taking the plates from me.

"Don't worry about it, Drew. Just relax. After all, it's your birthday," I said and playfully patted his shoulder wondering why he seemed to be in a bad mood.

Turning my attention back to my in-laws, we joked around as Amie pulled her hair up and lit the grill. Taking a sip of wine, she sang ebulliently, "Today is your birthday! It's my birthday too, yeah!" and we all laughed hard at her attempt.

As usual, she was the life of the party. She and Falene had been in competition to see who could give the biggest and best birthday gifts. That day was no exception; Amie's gift bag for Drew stood four feet tall and was stuffed with new sporting equipment. She excitingly presented it to Drew.

"How's my twin sister?" he suddenly blurted out when he stood and stumbled toward Amie spilling his plate of food on the patio.

Amie rolled her eyes and glanced at Seth, who sat undisturbed and potbellied eating chips and dip.

Amie and I moved to clean the spill concerned about Drew's uncharacteristic behavior. Mia and Toby were playing in the back by the swing set without a care in the world when suddenly Drew shouted, "Who wants to have a good time?" as his hands raised to symbolize devil horns banging high up in the air but then conforming to play air guitar as he lowered his head and thrashed it up and down while sticking out his tongue to appear like Gene Simmons. Amie and I took hard gulps of wine, looked at each other baffled, and wondered what had possessed Drew to become so inebriated. Swaying side to side, he walked heavily down our driveway as if his shoes were filled with cement. "Hey kids, why don't you come over here and play some basketball?" he shouted slurring his words.

"Drew, just let them be," I said cautiously.

"Mind your own business, Nora!" he sternly demanded with a threatening look, and my expression froze as I stared at the stranger in front of me.

Mia and Toby didn't notice the callousness in Drew's tone and ran excitingly toward him. They grabbed the basketball and laughed as they dodged toward the hoop. Drew joined as if he were trying out for pro aggressively grabbing the ball back from Mia and carelessly bumping her to the ground. Toby, oblivious to his father's drunkenness, cheered and laughed as Mia was rolling away with a half-confused smile.

Observing the situation, Amie yelled out for Drew to join the adults in a card game instead. As we played, Drew walked in and out of our house several times acting more intoxicated with each return, loudly repeating his words, knocking over drinks, and falling when he tried to sit.

Before our guests even finished their meals, I excused myself and walked inside to get the birthday cake, and I thought it odd to find the basement door opened.

Raymond, sitting at the table, said, "He's so weak, just like his mother. I don't know why I even bother with that boy."

Wanting to wrap up the party early at that point, I hurried back to our guests for a rushed birthday song and quick goodbyes.

CHAPTER 8

Choose your life's mate carefully. From this one decision will come 90 percent of all your happiness or misery.

—H. Jackson Brown Jr.

The company had left. I was cleaning and growing tired from the work even though the party had been small.

"Drew, are you okay? What got into you today? You were acting belligerent," I said feeling irritated.

"Are you accusing me of drinking?" he lashed out. Instantly his spark of anger ignited into a whirlwind of fury. "I don't drink that skunk spray!" he shouted at me in a barbaric charging stance.

"Drew, lower your voice. Toby's right down the hallway," I said bewildered. "I know you've been drinking, and you need to calm down." I spoke sternly and wondered how concerned I should have been. Trying to calm down a bit, I turned away and took a drink of water hoping for the moment to somehow suppress on its own.

But Drew cocked his hand back and slapped the water bottle out of my mouth lacerating my upper lip. I recoiled as he became more aggressive. "Do you really think I was drinking, woman?"

I gasped as he forced my back against the kitchen counter. His face was so close to mine that our noses were almost touching. The stench of alcohol suffocated the space between us. I stepped out from the side with hands in front of my body palms down as if to suggest surrender. "Drew, you're scaring me. Whatever's going on in your mind, please stop it," I implored, but my request didn't change him as he shoved me into the back door and I fell to the ground. Fear imprisoned my thoughts over his unimaginable intent. "Please stop," I said as excruciating throbs rose from my forearm, but somehow, my pleading seemed only to encourage Drew to scream louder.

He grabbed me off my feet and threw me down again and again and again like a rag doll until finally I curled my body forward and landed on the floor in a fetal position trying to guard myself from going through the glass window behind me. Drew grabbed a kitchen chair and smashed it against the wall barely missing my head. He flipped the kitchen table over as if it were made of paper instead of solid wood. It struck my ribs. I heard a crack. He screamed, "Come on, Nora! You're not so tough!"

I remained still. With my head between my knees, I squeezed my eyes shut. I silently prayed that Toby couldn't hear this abuse and wouldn't come out from the shower too soon to witness this.

After a moment, I slowly unwrapped my hands from the top of my head, raised my face, and stood. Drew looked dazed and seemed as though he'd suddenly realized what he was doing. I calmly walked out of the room. Drew followed. Within a few steps, he fell into the closet and broke the door off one hinge. He then tore it from the remaining hinges and tossed it down the hall. I knew he wasn't going to stop as he shoved me from behind, and I needed to get into an area where there was no glass, so I dove onto the couch. He reached down and tore my necklace from my neck and pounced on top of me like a wildcat pressing down so forcefully into my flesh that I could have bet his fingers would go straight through my chest.

Finally rolling out from underneath, I sat on the floor with my back tightly against a far wall. I was wide eyed as I contemplated the situation, I told Drew I needed to clean up outside. I was hoping he was too drunk to realize I'd already cleaned up outside. At any moment, our sweet, five-year-old son would be getting out of the shower, and if he saw what was going on, he would put himself in the middle and directly in harm's way.

Drew looked disoriented as he stumbled over the coffee table. I rushed out the back door having grabbed my cell phone knowing I had only seconds to dial 911 as I approached the side of our house. I whispered fretfully to the dispatcher, "My husband's after me! Please hurry!" I rattled off our address as she asked questions and pleaded with me to stay on the line. "I can't! He's after me, and he's in a rage!" Panicking, I hung up hoping she had heard the information correctly.

I heard the back door open. *He's coming.* I was consumed by the dread of his wrath. I had to get to the front of the house because the only window in the bathroom faced the backyard, and if Toby was still in there, he wouldn't be able to see what was going on.

Drew slammed the door opened against the rail of the stoop as he stumbled outside. Charging, he yelled, "Who're you talking to?" He chased me. His face was as red as the flames of fire, and in his bone-chilling tone, he yelled, "Bring 'em on! I'll kill 'em all!"

I felt for certain he was going to kill me. *God help me!* I repeated in my head as I began to move slower trying to catch my breath. I knelt on the side of my driveway panting. Crouching forward and avoiding eye contact, I wanted to appear small and harmless. With my hands grasping my knees, I kept quiet hoping he would see that I did not want to engage in any physical conflict.

Drew stood conspicuously tense under the light of the moon and arched his giant figure backward. His wide chest protruded toward the night sky. Clenching his fists stiffly downward, he contoured into a behemoth over me. "I'm going to *kill youuuu!*" he screamed with such profound, deafening hatred that I thought Toby would surely find me dead by the hands of his father. Of all the things I could have cared about that moment, I was mortified knowing his voice was reverberating throughout our quiet neighborhood.

Sobbing and shaking with terror, my heart pounded hard in my chest like the blow of a hammer striking steel. I wondered if I would suffer some kind of sudden emotional stroke. Just then, three police cruisers arrived. They commanded us to show our hands. I raised mine immediately. Drew looked at me with glaring eyes and smugly asked, "Are you kidding me?"

His feet remained a firm fixture to the ground as he lowered his chin displaying eyes as black and as cold as death. He turned to the officers like a lunatic curling his upper lip and cocking his head back. His torso leaned forward, and in a half-circle, he howled, "Come and get *meeee!* I'll take the entire police force down!"

An officer instructed Drew to get on the ground. He relented in a forward charging stance with bulging veins and muscles protruded through his clothing. He screamed as his body transformed into a possessed demon. "Bring it on! Bring it *on!*" The officers unbuckled their holsters, aimed at Drew's chest, and one of them pulled the trigger.

CHAPTER 9

Tasers paralyzed Drew to the asphalt. The officers approached him and handcuffed him. After a few minutes, Drew stood. Limp at first, he then attempted to thrash his large body around like a rabid animal as he tried to resist getting into the back of the cruiser.

While he was being restrained, Officer Melendez escorted me back into our house, where we found Toby standing outside his bedroom door in his dinosaur pajamas proudly proclaiming in his small voice, "Daddy! I'm done with my shower! Daddy, where are you? Come and say goodnight."

I slowly walked down our dim hallway to meet him. Officer Melendez followed.

"Hi! What are you doing here?" Toby asked as he stood smelling like candy apple soap.

Carefully intervening, I answered as calmly as I could, "Well, this is one of Daddy's friends. He stopped by to wish Daddy a happy birthday."

Toby replied, "Okay." Then with his bedroom light remaining off, I tucked him in hoping he didn't feel my trembling.

"This has to be a quick goodnight because we still have some company from the party," I explained. I pulled his blanket close to his chin and stared down at his innocent, sweet face trying to regain some sense of being alive.

"There was a hole, in the center of the earth. It was a very big hole, just waiting for you. And in this hole was a very big star, and this star was waiting for you. And in this star was a very bright light, and this light was waiting for you. And then one day, this very wise boy, he took this light and sprinkled it around. And around and around—and around and around—and around he went, for the whole world to see," I sang to Toby.

I sucked blood from the inside of my lip before smoothing aside a small auburn wave from his forehead to give him a tender goodnight kiss. I followed with my thumb wiping away any possible trace glad for the darkness of his room.

After I gently closed his bedroom door, Officer Melendez asked if anyone else was inside our house as he intrusively walked throughout.

"There isn't," I replied.

Dreadfully, I returned to the kitchen and struggled as I turned the table right side up stabilizing a cracked leg. I collected the only two scattered chairs still safe to use. As we sat, I caved with overwhelming emotions.

After some inquiring, we were met by Officer Bache, who explained that Drew would be spending at least one night in jail. "Your husband keeps repeating himself in the back of the cruiser telling us that he isn't a bad guy, he's just having a hard time because his father had left him after his mother died. Do you know what he's talking about, Mrs. Greyson?"

"No."

Melendez continued to seek out details for what seemed like hours. Bache took photos of my bloody lip, right forearm, and rib cage.

"Would you like to receive medical attention?" Melendez asked, but I declined.

The last thing I wanted was to risk Toby becoming suspicious. I didn't know about the several deep fingerprint bruises on my chest and back until the next day when I showered.

About an hour and a half into the investigation, Raymond called to tell me that Drew had called them from jail. "What happened?" he asked in a panicked outburst.

In less detail, I explained that Drew had become violent toward me and that I'd had to protect myself and Toby by calling the police.

"I asked Drew if you and Toby were okay, but he couldn't remember. I won't be bailing Drew out. You can count on that."

"I have to go. The officers are still here, Raymond."

"Could I speak to one of them?"

"No." I hung up bewildered over Drew's egregiously vacuous state.

Drew was charged with third-degree assault, disorderly conduct, interfering with a police investigation, and resisting arrest. While he was being fingerprinted in the booking area, with his chin lowered and eyelids raised, he muttered, "When he showed up, I was ready to blow."

"Here's my card," Melendez said handing one over along with information on how to get help with domestic violence. That's when it started to sink in. I was suddenly a victim of domestic violence. How had this happened? After sixteen years of being together, thirteen years married, and never having experienced anything even remotely close to this before, I was labeled as a victim of domestic violence just like that, and I'd never seen it coming.

CHAPTER 10

The officers left me sitting alone in dismay and pondering the train wreck. I noticed Drew's cell phone on top our kitchen counter. I turned it on and looked through his text messages for clues that could have suddenly transformed my supposedly loving husband into an unrecognizable, deleterious monster.

"I got it, and don't worry, I won't tell her," Raymond had texted Drew.

"Thanks. I deserve a drink on my birthday, and she doesn't need to know everything I do," Drew had responded.

"I understand. I'll bring the whiskey and sneak it to you."

Also in Drew's phone, I found a message from some girl: "Thanks for the chat. Talk to you tomorrow." That sounded like no big deal, but it was kind of odd because the previous year, he had mentioned how perfect she looked but then never brought her up again. I didn't know Drew was getting personal enough with her to communicate with her on what appeared to be a regular basis. Maybe it wouldn't have seemed so odd had I known.

I placed his phone down and shook my head. Tears streaked through bloodstains on my face as I thought about how odd it felt to have had the need to look through his phone. Something I'd never done before. He had a connect-the-dot security pattern that wasn't hard to figure out, but I wish I hadn't had to do it.

My arms dropped onto the kitchen table as a web of disbelief enveloped me. My clothes clung to my body with moist sweat, and only the sound of a clock's ticking cut through the silence. Time wouldn't be able to erase a time like this even though I wished it could. I wondered whose life this was. It wasn't mine.

Before that night, Drew and I had never spent a full twenty-four hours apart since our first date back in 2001. Now, as the order that the officer handed me stated, we would be forced apart by law for at least a few months.

It was 2:00 a.m. I walked to the closet door that was lying on the floor in the hallway. I found a glue bottle and pieced the small broken parts of shattered door back together so our house would appear normal when Toby woke up. Enervation started to settle in. I'd go to bed hoping to wake and find this had all been just a terrible nightmare.

CHAPTER 11

Day 2

I confronted Raymond.

"Drew asked me to get him a bottle of whiskey for his party because he said he was inviting friends. I told him I would, but then I felt uncomfortable because I knew you'd never approve of having hard liquor around children, so I told Drew I wouldn't get it for him," Raymond rushed to tell me.

"He'll need a ride from the courthouse, and that ride wouldn't be provided by me, nor will he be allowed to return to this house except for one time to retrieve his belongings," I stated.

By afternoon's end, Raymond was notified that Drew was out of the holding cell and roaming the courthouse city block barefoot. With all the intensity from the previous night, I hadn't noticed he hadn't been wearing shoes.

In attempt to redirect the conversation, I insisted on not telling Toby about his father's arrest. "We'll tell him that he's going to stay with you for a little while because you're not feeling well. Toby will believe it because he knows you have a hard time walking. I hope you'll reiterate this to Drew," I suggested decisively.

From beneath untold shame, Raymond reluctantly complied with my request.

CHAPTER 12

I was relieved to find that I could conceal all signs of my injuries under my clothes before Toby saw me in daylight though that required wearing a long-sleeve shirt on a hot, muggy day. I sat him down and explained that our police officer friend would be stopping by our house with his daddy to help him with his suitcases.

"Mommy, how long will Daddy be gone?" Toby asked sadly through big, brown eyes.

"I'm not sure, but Raymond really needs Daddy right now," I replied matter-of-factly.

"Okay, Mommy." Toby sighed.

I packed Drew's belongings to avoid a prolonged visit, planned a time for the meeting, and assured that Officer Melendez would escort Drew on site to witness and protect. When they arrived, everyone was civil. Drew reflected his usual calm self again even halfway flashing that smile that once stole my heart, but it was a craven shortcoming of a tainted Prince Charming at best.

Raymond and Falene distracted Toby with video games. I asked Drew to show me how to operate the wet vac we used when the basement flooded during heavy storms. He agreed, and with Officer Melendez following behind, we descended to the basement.

Tiptoeing around large puddles that consumed the ground, Drew indicated how to hook up the sump pump. I refused to make eye contact with him. With my chin lowered, I blankly focused on the ground and noticed him walking awkwardly. I dismissed the sight with indifference.

Once back upstairs, Drew got on his knees, hugged Toby, and told him he loved him.

"I love you too, Daddy. Will you call me tonight?" Toby asked sadly.

"Yes I will. I'll definitely call you. I love you so much," Drew said as they hugged.

When Drew stood, Raymond handed him a set of keys. He brushed past to a new, bright-orange muscle car with custom rims and a thick black stripe down the center of its hood, roof, and trunk. I cast Raymond a disagreeable look.

"The car was a surprise present for his birthday," Raymond stated looking culpable. "I bought Amie one last year," he added nervously.

The sun was beating down as we walked outside. Officer Melendez in his semi-permanent frown pulled me aside and dourly reinforced the rules of the restraining order. "Drew cannot be in contact with you after today until your next court date, when the judge decides the ruling. If I ever drive by here and see him, he'll automatically be spending five to ten years in prison for violating this order. Do you understand these conditions Mrs. Greyson?"

I swallowed hard. "Yes sir."

Raymond asked for a copy of the restraining order.

"No," I replied firmly.

"Well, we just feel so involved," Falene said as she hung from Raymond's side while he exaggerated the wobbliness of his cane.

Holding his stern gaze on me, Melendez ignored them before going to his cruiser.

I sat on our front steps and stared at Drew's taillights long after they were out of sight before returning to the basement to clean the puddles. I operated the equipment as he had demonstrated, and once the vac was full, I removed the lid to prepare to pour the water into the sump pump pit, and there it was. The previous night, I had searched the entire house to find out what Drew had been drinking and how much but had found nothing. Now in plain sight, a bottle of Fireball whiskey with only half an inch remaining on its bottom was floating in the wet vac tub of bubbly, filthy-brown basement water. The bottle was so huge it almost reached across both ends of the bucket's interior walls. A picture of a red devil flaring flames from the label stared up at me as the last drop of watery muck slapped down cutting through the stillness. Moving particles contrasted in an angled ray of sunlight that struck through a short window. With a single bare hand I reached into the grime, snatched the bottle and studied it as if it would speak dark secrets before it slipped away from my grip and shattered into jagged pieces across the concrete floor.

Just a few minutes earlier when Drew had been illustrating how to use the wet vac, he had never fully removed its lid; he had only verbally explained and pointed out how to detach the clips from the tubs base. Neither Officer Melendez nor I knew that the secret hiding place would be the same place of the demonstration, but I was sure Drew knew, and I could only imagine his uneasiness as he stood over his concealed, deceiving liquid courage.

CHAPTER 13

Day 3

The arrest happened on a Sunday. Officer Melendez's and Drew's visit occupied Monday. By Tuesday, I was back at work not missing a single scheduled day or telling anyone about what had transpired.

Raymond and Falene phoned while I was on my way. They worked like Velcro—one side completely useless without the other. Solemnly, I expressed how uncanny my life suddenly felt.

"Well, Drew has a swollen foot," Raymond replied ignoring my distress.

That explained why he had been limping. Without offering any insight, I suddenly recalled an officer stomping Drew's foot while struggling to control him during the arrest.

"And I wish you wouldn't have called the police because now Drew has to go through all these problems. We don't handle things by dialing 911 in our family," he added revealing the audacity conducive to victimizing Drew.

"How could you say that? Toby and I are the victims, not Drew!"

I thought about the night Ruby died. But I said nothing.

"Are you going to stay married to Drew?" Falene asked.

"There's no way I could answer that this early," I replied in a stiff voice.

"Well, there must have been *something* that made him do this to you, Nora," Raymond said. Raymond's amplification of "something" suggested he actually meant *This must be your fault, Nora.* "Just so you know, I'm getting advice from my lawyer."

"She doesn't want to hear that. She wants to feel valued enough to be respected," Falene said with an inflated accent that ended in a high-pitched nervous laugh as if she had just won a brownie point in their never-ending game of good cop bad cop.

"Thank you, Falene. I'm sitting right here," I said running low on patience and realizing this was the second time I had snipped at her.

"It's okay, darling." Raymond panicked as if my barely made response might have permanently damaged her world.

Maybe it was the intrusion that annoyed me. Maybe it was the fact that Falene was only five years older than Drew, married only one year to Raymond, and insisted on his constant reassurance that she came first in their weird family circle. Maybe it was because she acted more fragile than a robin's egg regardless of anyone's approach.

Thick silence wedged between us.

"Yesterday when we were at your house, Officer Melendez told me it was best for a third party to be present once Drew was allowed to see you again, so maybe Amie should be there during those visits," Raymond said.

I laughed at his foolish comment. "There's no way Officer Melendez said that," I replied aggravated at his continued attempt to connive me.

"*Ooo*," Falene said.

"*Ooo*," Raymond followed as of an echo to try to shame me for sticking up for myself.

"I found the bottle. I need to ask you again. Did you buy it for him?"

"No," they both said.

"Okay then. Goodbye, I have to work." I hung up. I didn't think I could trust them anymore.

Resting my elbows on my desk, I took a deep breath and leaned the soft part of my closed fist against my forehead.

I looked up the charge from our joint bank account for discrepancies. Before the party, Drew had purchased wine and ice for our guests, and the charge was $38.95. I wasn't sure about the price of the whiskey, but I planned to do some investigating.

Regardless of Raymond's aim to scrutinize, I wouldn't allow him to convince me that Drew had a right to put his hands on me. Not ever. And I'd never regret calling for help that night. Never before had any man laid a finger on me, and I refused to tolerate it.

I stared out the window frightened of this mental image of an empty shell that used to be my husband. My husband that for our entire relationship had never failed to leave little notes for me to wake up to in the morning telling me that he loved me and to have a nice day. My husband who planted beautiful gardens and kept our yard immaculate, spontaneously bought me roses, held me tight, and told me he thought I was beautiful even after sixteen years. My sweet, gentle husband who took such good care of our son filling his life with so much joy and laughter—He was Toby's hero, the beam of love in his heart and the smile on his face. What in the world had happened to my husband?

CHAPTER 14

Day 4

I printed pictures of my bruises especially those I hadn't seen the night of the arrest. I also printed screen shots of the text messages between Drew and Raymond. My ribs still ached, and my forearm was throbbing, but the inside of my mouth had healed.

I removed the "No Contact" portion of the restraining order. Drew was still restricted from our property and could not assault, threaten, abuse, harass, follow, or stalk me, but it felt impossible for Toby to not talk to or see his father at all. That's why I requested the change. It wasn't because I was no longer afraid or suddenly trusted Drew. I did it for Toby.

I spoke to Drew for the first time since he had picked up his belongings. I asked him to meet Toby and me in public as required by the restraining order. The following Sunday, we arrived as soon as the mall opened. Toby ran ahead and jumped into his dad's arms "I miss you so much, Daddy!"

"I miss you too, Toby," Drew replied lifting him in the air.

"Why don't you go and play in the courtyard while I talk to Mommy? I'll be sitting right over there watching you, okay?"

"Okay, Daddy!"

Toby ran off. My eyes met Drew's for the first time in what felt like a century. I had a tense lump in my throat. I was in an emotional trance. Silent tears streamed down on me and down on Drew as we stood a few feet from each other.

"My job is okay. Please don't worry about that. And I'm attending meetings to get the help that the court ordered," Drew said.

"I don't understand how you could have done this to us. My mind and my heart are so filled with confusion and pain that I'm almost numb to the physical wounds. I've never seen you like that before. I thought you were going to kill me." My own words gave me chills.

"I would never do that, Nora," Drew said dolorously taking a step toward me as if wanting to comfort me and erase all that had happened. I took a step back. I don't think he realized that in his moment of out-of-control rage, yes, he definitely could have killed me. Or maybe he just didn't remember all the details of his horrifying behavior.

I walked to a bench set aside for parents. Drew followed and sat on an adjacent bench. We remained like strangers with a million miles between us. As I watched our innocent boy skip through a soft world of dinosaur jungle, my mind struggled to recollect missed signs that could have helped me foresee this nightmare. The only time that held a mild comparison was several years prior, while we were still living in our apartment.

One Friday afternoon during my last work break, Drew called to tell me he was cooking a new recipe for dinner. After a long work week, I hinted that it would be nice to share a glass of wine with our meal. I looked forward to the last few hours of my day to end, but when I arrived home, I was disappointed to find him obnoxiously drunk. I confronted him, and he denied it pointing to a bottle of wine on our kitchen table that was missing only a single glass. Feeling annoyed with his rambling repetitive lie, I went for a walk. When I approached the end of our lot, I noticed the lid to our dumpster opened and spotted a large empty bottle of the same wine still wet but completely empty on top of a pile of trash. Drew had drunk that entire bottle in less than the one-hour difference it took between his arriving home and my arriving home. So he did indeed have only one glass of wine, from a second bottle that was.

Later that evening, although nothing physical took place, Drew became verbally aggressive toward me just enough to make me uncomfortable but not make me feel threatened. I packed a bag, grabbed my keys, and left to stay at a hotel for the night. I considered divorcing him back then, but there I was faced with one bad night against seven great years together.

The next day, I gave Drew an ultimatum—it was either me or alcohol, but either way, I was not going to stay with him if he didn't get help. He got help, but it was temporary. Nevertheless, only once every few years during the past nine years had Drew touched alcohol, and when he did, he did it secretively as if he felt shameful.

CHAPTER 15

Day 5

The woman who answered the domestic violence help line clearly had experience. She didn't hesitate to tell me it would happen again. After hearing this confirmation, all I could do was cry.

"Not only will this happen again, but it will be much worse," she explained. "Things will be great for a while. He'll charm you, and then he'll hurt you. Domestic violence isn't just physical; it's mental and emotional too. There are three stages of domestic violence. They are the buildup, the blow up, and then the honeymoon."

After hearing that I was determined to figure out how the buildup had happened for Drew. I had no doubt that she was right. If I took Drew back, he would be as perfect as he had been during the first several years of our marriage, but what about a year from now, or five years from now, after the honeymoon stage had worn off? The problem was that the more I came across as forgiving and accepting, the quicker he'd feel safe to not only repeat his abusiveness but take it to the next level.

She offered tips on how to protect myself and Toby.

- Decide on a place to go that he doesn't know about if you need to leave your home.

- Practice getting out safely—which doors and windows to use.
- Inform one or more neighbors about the violence, and ask them to call the police if they hear a disturbance coming from your home.
- Make sure your child knows how to call 911. You can now text 911 if talking isn't safe.

I was thankful and relieved that I was already practicing some of this advice. She asked if I noticed a pattern or some kind of sign of abuse in the past, but nothing major stood out.

When we had first started dating, Drew had been a little jealous of my friends, but he had never threatened me or spoke violently. To ease his mind, I spent every free moment with him. I was with him more than I was with my own thoughts. Looking back, that wasn't a good thing. What once seemed flattering suddenly felt controlling.

Early in our relationship, I heard a story about his abusing his ex-girlfriend, flipping over a table at her while he was drunk. I had never seen that violent side of him. In fact, he was always the exact opposite, so I brushed it off as Drew must have been mistaken for someone else. Until over a decade later, when that warning became my reality.

As I thought about his behavior, I remembered a few times that I should have considered much more carefully. The first was when I helped him pack up his old apartment to move in together. I noticed empty beer cans under his bed. I thought that was a little strange, but I eventually brushed it off as typical early twenties male behavior. But why hide it, I thought?

Another time was a few months after we started living together. One night, he drank too much and just stood in our living room and screamed about his father leaving him while ripping his shirt off his body for what appeared to be no connection with the present. That was the first time I witnessed him acting aggressively, but he made no attempt to be violent with me.

After that was the time I mentioned previously when I left him for the night.

And then there was the present.

When I examined the history, I saw that each occurrence had taken an additional depth toward pushing the limit, and although these occasions were few and far between, they never stopped. From the last warning sign until the present existed several beautifully lived years with a soft-spoken, kind gentleman.

I had never approved of those deceiving moments, but each time I felt was an isolated event; I also thought I had too much invested in the relationship to give it up. I felt that if I divorced him, I could just about guarantee that he would drink regularly, and the thought of what might happen to Toby if he and his father were alone during one of Drew's out-of-control drinking episodes frightened me. Who would be there to protect Toby? And if I got full custody of Toby, how would he ever be the same emotionally without his father? So I could either stay married to Drew and when it happened again have a plan, or let Drew go and always worry about Toby's emotional well-being and safety when I wasn't around.

I knew what I had to do as a mother. As long as I was with Drew, at least I'd have some control most of the time. But I'd have to form and maintain a very precise plan of survival and escape for when Drew did come home to live. I had to make sure I was prepared because as much as I hoped this would never happen again, I knew it would.

CHAPTER 16

Our personalities and identities are shaped by the roots of our youth, regardless of desire or detest.

—Nora Greyson's journal

Day 6

I think I can journal forever and still come to the same conclusion—that we are a product of our childhood environments. Either we are going to revolve around it or evolve from it.

I recall Drew talking in detail about the night he saw his mother drinking in secret just before she died. Raymond chased her in a state of rage as she screamed and ran to her car while Drew and Amie hid fearfully in the back of a dark closet where they had found shelter several times before.

After that final night, Raymond would go away on long business trips usually without warning or even saying goodbye, sometimes staying gone for several months without any contact, one time for over a year. Drew spent so much time despising moments like that that he'd become like them. Toby is five years old. The same age Drew was when his mother died.

The buildup wasn't a buildup of current events at all for Drew. It was always there, born through the abandonment of his father, and because Raymond viewed therapy as a weakness, Drew and Amie were denied any chance of a proper emotional recovery, and as if they were still trying to win their father's approval, they continued to refuse help into their adulthood. Now, the slightest aggravation in Drew's everyday life piled on top causing him to become a walking time bomb.

CHAPTER 17

Day 7

Last night, I had a dream about Drew's mother, Ruby Greyson.

During my dream, she was lying on a stretcher inside my grandmother's house. (Dreams have a way of making strange combinations.)

From a faraway place, our family members huddled and whispered to each other with distraught expressions. I was alone inside my grandmother's small walk-in storage room sitting on a stool. I heard Ruby on the other side of the door whimpering.

"I'm so sorry he did this to you. I'm so sorry. I'm so sorry." Her voice was strained as it trailed off into an unrecognizable audio undertone with profound, lingering sorrow.

Slowly, I walked out of the room to her side and wrapped my arms around her. Our surroundings faded to a soft white as if we were floating in an infinity of peaceful nothingness where only the two of us existed. She wrapped her arms around me and put her mouth against my ear. With struggling intensity, she forced herself to cry out as if all her remaining strength was given up just to assure that I heard these last words: "I'm so sorry he did this to you. I'm so very sorry. I love you."

Even though she visually appeared to be physically weak while the rest of her body lay still, her arms felt so lovingly strong, safe, and warm; they reassured me of the genuineness of her intent.

I never spoke a word in my dream. All I felt was love. I woke in the bliss of peaceful serenity. I wondered if my sorrow had become so knowing that it had reached heaven.

CHAPTER 18

Day 8

I stopped by the liquor store that I had sent Drew to the day of his party, and this is what I discovered. A 750 milliliter bottle of that whiskey, the size I'd found in the tub of the dry vac that Drew drank the day of his party, was 66 proof, 33 percent alcohol, and cost $18.99. Ice was $2 per bag. The two bottles of wine cost $32, so the total should have been $34.00 plus tax. Maybe Drew bought a nip while he was in the store. Regardless, the total cost on my credit card was less than a cost that would have included the Fireball whiskey. I had checked our bank statements and other credit card statements but saw no other charges or cash withdraws. I felt certain that Raymond had lied about buying the Fireball for Drew. Maybe it was guilt because his decision reflected the results of that night. Either way, he had lied.

CHAPTER 19

Day 9

The day was warm, late in the spring season with leaves already displaying a thick variety of green throughout the wood that outlined the grassy plain beyond the groomed field.

We sat at the guidelines and cheered him on as he courageously gripped the baseball bat with anticipation. "Come on, Toby! Hit the ball!"

He smacked it a few feet in front. "Run!" we shouted jumping from our seats, and Toby flung the bat backward almost connecting with the catcher, who swiftly dodged out of the way.

When he was safely at first base, we stood and clapped and smiled as hard as two proud parents could. Toby smiled back squinting at us; the bright sun shone on his happy face. He offered silly jumps up and down while guarding the base.

Knowing the treat ahead, Toby ran with aspiration from the dugout into his father's arms, and Drew tossed him up high onto his shoulders. Toby bounced and giggled and bent down sideways to spy, and Drew reached with one finger to touch that freckle on Toby's nose, and Toby playfully placed his small hands over his father's eyes as if to play peek-a-boo. Drew securely grasped

Toby's knees and gave a twirl around in amusement, and Toby and I laughed with delight.

I swung his sporting bag over my shoulder, and we walked to our favorite ice cream stand Drew and I hand in hand and Toby still on top of Drew. I ordered my usual vanilla cone dipped in cherry topping. Toby and Drew ordered their favorite brownie sundaes smothered in hot fudge. We sat at a picnic table under the gazebo where lake waters met ducks that swam in a harmonious line. We watched in wonder and savored our treats as the sun softened away from the sky. As it was in the beginning, it is now in this memory and has been every day of our life together. Love.

I knew Toby really missed moments like this. Ordinary moments we used to take for granted. Moments like family movie night, fishing trips, or flying kites at the beach at sunset.

It had been a few days since we'd heard from Drew. Toby often said he missed him and especially during dinner time, and that particular night, he looked as though he was going to cry. He was so accustomed to our daily family meals together and the closeness he shared with his father. As Toby stared down at his plate of untouched food, I tried to assure him that everything would be okay even though I was sure it wouldn't be.

Toby pushed his plate aside and buried his face in the crease of his elbow resting on the table and cried.

CHAPTER 20

Day 10

At work, I interviewed a new graphic designer for the upcoming season. Her name was Josie. She was an older woman with a comedic side, and only God knew how long it had been since I'd experienced laughter.

Josie told me that she had buried her mother, Rita, two days previously and was speaking to her spirit. She said to Rita's spirit while driving to meet me, "Things were always good between us, weren't they, Mom?" Just then, a white car passed her; on its side were the words "Rita's Compassionate Care." Josie looked at me in a peculiar way. "There are no coincidences in life, and God knows when to tap your shoulder. Anger is a terrible thing. It eats a person up inside, and I like my insides. I don't want them eaten." (Her comedic side I guessed.) "There is only one thing people get mad about. That's when they don't get their way," she said.

I said that some people were just angry people, and she agreed. She said that she used to be one of them but that now, when she had an angry thought, she made sure it was her first thought, not her last. Then she'd ask herself if it was something she could control and if it was worth the anger. Then she'd decided that life was too short and let it go.

It was very unusual to have a stranger speak to me this way especially during a job interview, but for some reason, I felt compelled to listen. Josie was a very down-to-earth, genuine woman however peculiar as that may sound considering her bold statements that derailed her from her professionalism.

No one at my work knew what was going on in my life and especially not a potential new hire. I was always mindful about separating private matters from work to not draw any attention to my personal life, and I have never left my work phone number for contact or posted on social media, so there was no way leakage could have occurred.

Josie worked with us for only three months and then disappeared. Throughout that time, she often stopped in my office to share a joke or talk to me about anger and forgiveness. Perhaps she was an angel of some sort. Perhaps she was God's way of tapping my shoulder. I liked to think so.

CHAPTER 21

Day 14

I sat as still as slate in cogitation with sweat melting from my forehead when suddenly a tender hand wrapped around my shoulder from behind and thick auburn waves came to rest on my chest. "I'm hot, Mommy" Toby moaned softly, his face highlighted with sun-brushed freckles.

I was relieved for the interruption. I changed into my bathing suit and a T-shirt over my top to hide the lingering fingerprint bruises on my chest and back that were at that point a muted grayish-yellow.

We walked past the remains of our garden that was starting to weed over, Toby with his hands full of water blasters and mine holding a bag stuffed with pool towels, drinking water, a container of fresh fruit, and sun block, and we drove off to refresh at our town pool. Spotting some school friends there, Toby hurried to join them in water activities and I submitted to the relief of having a moment of normality.

Afterward, we met Drew at an outdoor park so Toby could visit him. I didn't feel intense anger toward him as I had the previous week but instead relief that I needed to be around him only for a few hours and then I could go home. Alone.

"I miss you and Toby so much. I'm so sorry for all this. I can't eat. I can't sleep. I just want to make things right," Drew repented.

He used to despise men who abused women. At that point, he despised himself. He looked terrible—broken and shameful.

Toby looked up at his father with heavy brown eyes. "Daddy, please come home where you belong."

Drew seemed like he was about to cry. "Nora, you're the perfect woman for me, and I want nothing more than to be the perfect husband for you. I'm falling apart without you and Toby."

"I never would have wanted things to be this way, Drew. I'm sorry we weren't enough for you to be happy with on your birthday, but I'll never be sorry for protecting myself and Toby. I don't feel safe with you anymore. Some men do this to their wives regularly, and their wives take them back, bail them out even. I'm not that kind of wife."

"I know," Drew said looking down with regret.

He had had so much anger in him lately, I thought to myself. It came on so subtly that I didn't even know when it had started. For several months prior to his birthday party, he would leave for work in the morning in his usual way hugging me and Toby and wishing us a good day. He would continue to text and call on every break, but by the time he would return home, he would act like a different person. He was short with his words impatient and rude, but never violent.

He seemed to corroborate more when I was cold toward him, but it felt so unnatural and undesirable to have to be peremptory guarded this way. I'm the positive. He's the negative. Except I had to default to being negative to get positive results, and I didn't like that.

Jumping off a swing, Toby approached us. "I'm hungry."

Traveling in separate vehicles, we met for pizza. Drew seemed to be eating just fine. His insidious complaining included his saying how he didn't belong in "those" anger management classes because other people in his group had real anger issues and were not like him at all. When I asked Drew if he realized how much worse things could have ended, he changed his response. Switching the subject, he complained about how Falene was constantly prying into his life and how terrible her cooking was.

"I can't listen to this anymore," I said.

Looking out the window in disgust, I recalled having been forced overnight into a new life that I'd never signed up for and certainly had never seen coming. I spend my days lying about where Drew was to spare our reputation and to avoid the hassle of added attention. I pushed myself to be productive constantly hiding my tears at work and around Toby.

Meanwhile, Drew was looking like a loyal saint of a son who was making sacrifices to help his crippled father. How dare he complain about Falene's cooking when his five-year-old had been wavering through such confusion and distress trying his best to move on with school and his own life with the sudden absence of his father? How could Drew have so carelessly not considered the scarring effects on Toby? But I said nothing. To my relief, Drew stopped complaining.

As I departed with Toby, I became overwhelmed with sadness.

Later that night, Drew sent me his first personal text message saying, "'Night." I didn't respond. I hoped he didn't think we had been on some sort of date that day.

CHAPTER 22

Day 16

To date, I've spoken to only two people about that night. The first was Kelsa, my close childhood friend who would be visiting from out of state for the first time in over a year. She didn't come because of what had happened to me; she had planned this visit several times before, but it hadn't worked out. God knew exactly when to bring her back, and I was thankful that she'd be staying with Toby and me for a few weeks.

The second person I confined in was Leann, Kelsa's mother, who especially since I'd known her for practically my whole life doubled as a mother figure to me and was as bright as a fresh from the Mensa Society. She lived just a few blocks away. Spending time with her was like spending time with a world of knowledge.

The summer evening's breeze was refreshing, and it felt good to be with Leann among tikis and moonlight.

"Pray, Nora," she said. "Now is a time to really pray to God and keep a journal."

Leann was retired from her medical practice and had dedicated the past few years of her time to help care for patients at a dialysis center. She shared a heartfelt story with me about how God interceded during one of her shifts. She was assisting a patient when venous needle dislodgement occurred.

"Within minutes my patient experienced a significant amount of blood loss. Her pulse rate and blood pressure plummeted. Although unusual, this can be fatal. I just remember grabbing her hand and praying. And then I tried again, and the bleeding stopped. It was God, Nora. Never underestimate His power," Leann said as she shook her head in grateful recollection.

"My patients have to sit in their hospital chairs for four hours a day three days a week, and it was by the grace of God that I was able to come up with new sassy jokes to share in attempt to lift their spirits every visit. It's a tough life, Nora, and once patients are on dialysis, they can never come off it. If they did, they'd risk dying within forty-eight hours.

"This particular patient, the one who endured the dislodgement, is very special. Her name was Gracie, and she was my rock. Her inner strength was so unbreakable that it almost made me feel guilty to ever consider my own problems. It was always my responsibility to assure the best health to all my patients, but with Gracie, she became like another daughter to me. That's how fond I was of her. Everyone at the center was. I'm still in touch with her even after all these years even though I no longer dedicate my free time to the center. Sometimes, Nora, we learn the most and grow the most in inner strength through the ones who appear to be the weakest. Never judge a book by its cover. You could miss your pot of gold."

I let that soak in.

"Do you miss him?" she asked gently.

I thought about Leann's question. Surprisingly, I didn't think I missed him as much as I'd thought I would. I wondered if it was because for once I was in the control seat and was relieved to have time to myself. Or maybe it was because I'd felt emotionally and psychologically manipulated for so long that it had become my norm to tread through my days cautiously, and I hadn't realized that until lately. Maybe I'd lost some feelings for Drew, and my daily "I love you's" to him had become robotic instead of sincere. Maybe it was all the above.

I remember returning to work the weekend after Drew's party and sitting at my desk thinking, *This is it. I have to divorce Drew and be without him now.* I felt so alone. I wondered if that was missing someone or just being afraid to live without him because I'd done that for so long.

Other than that, truly missing Drew came and went in small spurts. It had been a few years since Drew had treated me with steady kindness, and that had worn my spirit thin. I could not allow myself to become lost in thoughts of how good he used to be before that. I did love him, or at least the memory of the man I thought I'd married. Either way, I knew I wasn't ready to let go of my marriage or prepared to take him back so soon.

Drew had been texting and calling me more than I was comfortable with. Not in a harassing way, but it was just more than I wanted him too, so I let him know that, and he agreed to slow down. He told me he just wanted to do whatever it took to make things right.

CHAPTER 23

∽

It is a place where a turtle may live, a time of day the sun spoke a soft song and the birds glided without care—where the smell of a fresh willow cleanses the broken path and an old friendship comforts the soul.

—Nora Greyson's journal

Day 19

Resting back on a white Adirondack chair that moved to the motion of water, I sipped my iced tea and watched Toby, who had just cast his fishing line into the lake.

"I'm going to catch the big one this time, Auntie Kelsa!" Toby said while stepping forward as he steadied himself like a funambulist.

It had been a very long year without Kelsa by our side, and I valued the time with her more than I would have a diamond ring. Toby always referred to her as Auntie Kelsa even though we weren't technically related. She had been the root of my calmness and the stability of my foundation since we were just about Toby's age, and I was at rest in her presence.

Kelsa lay on her towel on top of Leann's dock. "You can do it,

Toby!" she cheered confidently with a smile that could light up the entire town.

And a tug ignited a thrill, and a trout was flung aboard, and we approached it in correlation to our youth.

> It is a place where problems didn't stand a chance to manifest because we had us. It's home.
>
> —Nora Greyson's journal

CHAPTER 24

Day 26

I'd been a graphic designer for almost thirteen years and had recently encountered the nastiest customer yet. I'd made a mistake. I'd accidently approved her order without double-checking the sample, which left out important marketing information valuable to her business. This was something I've never overlooked before in the entire history of my career, and it resulted in my client's being unprepared for her grand opening she'd already advertised. I worked around the clock to create a knockoff that wouldn't be noticeable to any other human being but me, but unfortunately, that didn't change her outlook at all.

Mrs. Lurcher left several threatening messages and emails demanding my attention to this matter, and I gave her my attention and apologized each time. I tried to explain that when she had changed a part of her slogan, that had somehow erased the entire sentence, and our production department didn't inform me, but the truth didn't seem to deter her outlandish behavior. She screamed at me that I was a horrible person and a terrible designer and that she was going to write a blog about this awful experience and tell everyone what she thought of me. I kept trying to apologize to her, but I couldn't get a single word in. She just screamed over me and demanded to speak to the owner to challenge him not to pay me anything for her job. Day after day, she left several hateful messages demanding my attention and claiming I wasn't giving her any even though I pointed out to her during that one week, I documented sixteen emails, had had twelve phone call conversations with her, and had left her five voice mails.

Mrs. Lurcher's cruelty far exceeded my mistake, and yet I felt desperate for forgiveness especially since she was at that point refusing to pay. Feeling overwhelmed, I explained everything to my boss, and together, we tried one more time; we sent her another apology letter and let her know I hadn't made this mistake out of malice.

The next day, it was like a light switch. She was suddenly very nice; in all the following emails, she addressed me as "My Dearest Nora," and they were loaded with thank-yous and kindness. In addition, she sent me a referral and wanted to pay her bill in full even though her project wasn't finished. I couldn't figure out the purpose of her in my life when I was already dealing with so much at home until recently.

CHAPTER 25

Day 29

The air was stuffy in a small room where he sat beside a mound of files and a computer monitor. I entered for my court-appointed meeting with Marc, a family counselor, to give a statement and listen to his recommendations.

"Please sit, Mrs. Greyson." His thick hand gestured toward a worn, faux leather chair on tingy metal legs. He retreated behind his desk with a grave look and massaged a bulging button over his stained white shirt. He folded his arms over Drew's file and leaned forward heavily. "I've acquainted myself with your husband's records. At this point, I suggest he attends domestic violence classes." He spoke gruffly. The smell of old tobacco and stale coffee escaped from his stained mouth. I tried not to gag.

I agreed to Marc's suggestion, and I asked for Drew to continue with anger management classes.

"I have no desire to keep my husband from our son. It's not for Drew's sake but for Toby's. This has been very upsetting for him. Regardless of how I feel about Drew, I have to admit that up until this point, he had been a great father. I just want to be assured of Toby's safety."

Marc surveyed me with a narrow eye. He leaned back in his chair and tapped his desk top with his pencil. "You're a good mother," Marc stated genuinely as his eye stayed down in reflection. "Most people use their children as a way to retaliate, and it only hurts the kids."

"Thank you. I appreciate your sentiment."

We finalized by signing the documents. The next day, I learned that Drew had been dismissed from domestic violence classes. I phoned Marc immediately. "What happened? How did this get changed?" I asked in a panic.

"In all my many years' experience in dealings of domestic violence, time after time, the abuser walks into my office and says, 'This is all a misunderstanding. It was all her fault, and I'm not taking those classes,' but when your husband walked in, he said, 'This is all my fault. I'll never forgive myself for what I've done. What do you recommend I do to make sure I keep getting help and this never happens again? I want to make things right.' It got to the point that I had to tell him to just try to relax and give it some time. I don't usually say things like that to people. You should also know the domestic violence class costs four hundred dollars, and I don't think Drew needs that on top of anger management. Look, I can tell a fake from a sincere person. Drew attended more classes in three weeks than most people do in a year. I feel this was an isolated incident. It's completely up to you, Mrs. Greyson, but if Drew continues at the rate he's going and fulfills the class hour requirements, all charges against him will be removed and his record will be clean. He has no other past criminal records on file."

I thought about Drew's future. How would he ever be able to find a better job if he had a criminal record? In addition, Drew's pay had been significantly lower because of all the work hours he was missing to attend so many classes. Once again, I decided to go along with Marc's suggestion. After all, he was the professional.

Afterward, when I spoke to Drew about my concerns with the lack of money for our bills, he asked, "What did you think would happen when *you* did this?"

I froze. Once Toby was no longer in the room, I expressed concern for his words and reminded him that I'd never blame myself for his actions.

"I'm sorry, Nora. I didn't mean to say that. I know this is my fault. I'm just under a lot of pressure, but the classes are really helping. Falene is driving me up a wall. She's always in my business from the second I wake up until the second I go to sleep at night. She follows me around and asks me what I'm doing constantly. Amie keeps calling because she's having problems with Seth. She's been getting drunk a lot, and so has Raymond. I need to get out of here. It's too much stress."

That time, his complaining didn't annoy me. I agreed with him that he shouldn't be in that environment while he was trying to better himself, but I also knew that he never kept close enough friends to go anywhere else. However, I truly felt that in order for other areas of our relationship to improve, it was necessary for things to have come to a head, which forced this help into Drew's life, and I wasn't going to bail him out so soon.

There were so many things I hoped Drew could receive guidance for, things that I had fallen short in providing. I hoped he'd develop enough emotional strength to become capable of comforting and calming me and listening to me when I was having a bad day without getting angrier than me and threatening to take action against the person who was causing me grief.

When I'd first started dating Drew, back when I was in my twenties, I thought this behavior was flattering, honorable, and romantic, that a boy would go to such extreme to protect me. But I had seen how immature and dangerous this gesture was. It was almost as if he were constantly on guard for an opening to express his anger any way he thought he could get away with it. Drew has developed a new, definite, and unpredictable mean streak.

I hoped he'd learn to respect boundaries and makes lasting improvements instead of excuses. If Drew and I were having a disagreement, regardless if it was appropriate or not, he insisted on talking about it openly and on the spot even if Toby was in the room.

In spite of Raymond's behavior that night, Drew admitted that Raymond had bought the bottle of whiskey and had asked him to lie to me about it. That was expected considering Raymond's deceitful history. Unfortunately, Raymond was always more concerned about being popular than he was about doing the right thing.

CHAPTER 26

Day 34

A few days had passed since the meeting at family services, and my conversation with Marc kept repeating in my mind. I was feeling that Drew's absence was doing our marriage more damage than good, and I wondered if there would ever come a time when I felt certain that it would be okay for Drew to return home.

I asked him to meet me at the courthouse. Marc suggested my presence when Drew requested that the protective order be modified. That would help persuade the judge to become favorable to our agreement. Toby missed his dad terribly and wanted him home for his first day of school the next week. I missed him sometimes too though I hadn't told him that.

"I love you so much. I can't wait to come home to you and Toby," Drew said.

"I'm still upset about how you treated me during your birthday party. Maybe I should be over it by now, but I'm not. I'm nervous about your coming home."

As I expressed my feelings, Drew calmly thanked me for calling the police that night. "Nora, it was the right thing to do. I'm receiving very good help, and I feel like a completely different person now. I'm sorry I didn't get this help on my own before all this happened. I'm sorry I failed to realize how much anger I had been walking around with. I want you to know that I'm here for you and that everything will be okay."

It had been years since I'd heard Drew sound that way, and it filled me with hope.

I had lunch with Leann. For many years, she witnessed the strong family bond Drew, Toby and I shared. She asked, "Do you know how many times you should forgive someone you love? Always just one more time."

She reminded me that Drew by nature was a gentle soul, and she didn't think he had done this to be malicious.

CHAPTER 27

It's easy to judge. It's more difficult to understand. Understanding requires compassion, patience, and a willingness to believe that good hearts sometimes choose poor methods. Through judging, we separate. Through understanding, we grow.

—Doe Zantamata

Day 35

I woke to the reflection of Leann's advice. At work, I kept asking myself why this had ever happened to Drew and me when it seemed that we had had so much love for each other. Why was everything in my life so difficult to understand all of a sudden? My husband had hurt me beyond bruises, and I'd had the most difficult customers that year.

As the epiphany came to light, I realized I needed to completely forgive Drew. I was a strong wife, and I could overcome such things. For Toby's sake and for the sake of our family, I could forgive and take him back home without ever bringing this up again.

As I reflected on recent experiences with my previous designer, Josie, who didn't know me at all, frequently stopped into my office to talk to me about anger and forgiveness. The ruthless Mrs. Lurcher, who had shown me how it felt to desperately need forgiveness, Leann's words over lunch about love and forgiveness, and the professional sanction of Marc had me wondering what would become of me. I believed God had sent me all this to tell me I needed to forgive Drew, but I'd been too filled with anger and resentment that I hadn't seen the signs.

I asked Drew if he would meet me without Toby for the first time since we'd separated. He agreed. I was going to tell him I forgave him. He has said he was sorry a hundred times over, but I had just ignored him. I missed his smile, his smell, his touch, the way he loved me, and his dedication to our family and home. I loved him. And I couldn't wait for our family to be whole again.

CHAPTER 28

Though many of us take pride in how different we are from our parents, we are endlessly sad at how different our children are from us.

—Andrew Solomon, *Far from the Tree*

Day 36

When Drew and I met, I told him everything about what had happened the night of his party—from his sudden and unpredictable rage that had almost put me through our kitchen window to his being tased at the foot of our driveway by the police and my sucking the blood from my lip while putting Toby to bed.

Barely able to speak, Drew was genuinely distraught and shocked over what he had done especially when I showed him the photos of the damage he'd caused my body and our home. And then I allowed the story to be done.

As we sat at the park bench by the river, I placed my hands over his and told him I forgave him. He looked up and said he'd been praying for my forgiveness, and the word *praying* was not a usual part of Drew's vocabulary. At one point, I was certain I'd never be able to forgive Drew for any of this, but I realized that if I didn't forgive him, I'd be forever walking around with the same anger Drew had, and that was unacceptable.

I spoke to Drew at length about forgiveness and asked him to open his heart to forgiving his mother for dying, forgiving his father for constantly walking in and out of his life and not being there for him emotionally, and forgiving himself for his own wrongdoings even if he thought none of these people deserved it. It was a struggling conversation, but in the end, he thanked me. After we parted, he returned to Raymond's for a long overdue talk.

"I saw you and Mom that night, Dad. After you chased her out of the house, I looked out the window and saw Mom get into her car. Her head was bleeding. I know you hit her, Dad. I saw you. And I saw you punching her car as she drove off and ran your foot over. All these years, you told me it was a golfing accident that caused you to walk with a cane, but I knew the truth. And I know Mom was hysterical when she left our driveway and got into the car accident that killed her that night.

"I blamed you for a long time. I wanted to scream at you, but you weren't there, so my screams stayed inside. And when you were home, I was afraid to talk to you because I was afraid you would see all my ugly anger and leave again. But it didn't matter because you always left again anyway.

"As much as I hated you for what you did to Mom, I still didn't want to do anything to disappoint you, not any more than I already had, which felt like just me breathing was too much for you to deal with. I started to hold my breath until I passed out, but you never noticed. You just floated from one new wife to another, and I became a background annoyance of a past that you wished had never happened.

"You have no idea how many times I thought about the closeness we used to share before Mom died and how many nights I cried myself to sleep wondering why you kept leaving me, praying to God that you would love me again just so I could tell you how mad I was at you. I forgive you, Dad, because I can't live in your shadow of regret anymore. I wish you'd stop drinking and forgive yourself."

"Well well well, listen to you!" Raymond said. "Do you think you're smart all of the sudden with all that therapy you're getting? You're nothing but a liar and a spineless fool just like your mother. She always needed therapy ever since she gave birth to you and Amie. She couldn't handle it. What kind of a woman can't handle giving birth? You think you have a right to judge my drinking when you just did what you did to your own wife and kid? How dare you, Drew!"

"Dad, I learned all I know by watching you," Drew said calmly.

"After all I've done for you? After just buying you that car? You don't appreciate anything! Falene and I were just talking about changing our Will. We'll be removing you first thing tomorrow. You'll never see a single penny of your mother's inheritance mark my words, Andrew, and you need to get over your childhood. That was a long time ago. Your memory is terrible anyway, so stop making a mountain out of a molehill. Your mother died because she was weak. It was her own fault."

"You always make me feel like I have to earn you. Like me just being your son was never a good enough reason for you to love me. While I was getting married, you hosted a family reunion on the same day so you could be sure there would be no way I would show up and be sure I had few family members supporting me on my wedding day. What kind of a father does that? What did I ever do to you to make you feel so ashamed of me? What? You didn't think I knew about the reunion? You can't hide things like that, Dad, and you can't buy *me*."

"Get out of my house! I want to be left alone with my family anyway, which means Falene, not you! It's no wonder Nora doesn't want you back and your life has always been such a mess with the way you act. You deserve everything bad that's ever happened to you!"

"She does want me back. She just doesn't want me to be like you. Goodbye, Raymond."

Drew came home two days later after the judge honored the changes to the restraining order. Although he was still rejected by Raymond, he seemed auspiciously different and had much more self-control. I think he was relieved that he'd finally spoken his mind after all this time. He appeared lighter and authentically less angry. May God watch over us.

CHAPTER 29

Day 405

He ran with arms splayed freely, flannel and dark auburn locks of hair wafting in a crisp autumn breeze, and the bright glow of his big, brown eyes reflected the beauty of his youthful spirit.

"I want this one!" Toby hugged a huge pumpkin. "Can we put it in our wagon and take it home?"

Picking it up from the patch, Drew smiled and touched that favorite freckle on Toby's nose. Toby took charge of pulling the wagon past the corn maze, past the tall sunflowers that met me near the field of apple trees. Together, we gathered our supplies, hearts in hearts, hands in hands, and went home to make pie.

It had been a little over a year since my last entry, and life had been as wonderful as it could have been. Although I didn't think it was possible to completely forget the horrific experience I'd endured, I'd put it behind me. Drew's gentle, loving demeanor came back, and he was better than ever. He committed to staying away from Raymond and Falene, and I thought that their lack of negative emotional influence had helped Drew overcome his past.

"It's just you and me," I told him.

"You and me forever and ever, amen," he finished and pulled me close to kiss me on top of my head. And Toby remained the cheese. I couldn't have been more thankful for my family.

PART III

UNTITLED

CHAPTER 30

Death changes life instantly; whether through the death of a relationship or physical being, tiny or devastating, and whether acceptance takes place, or darkness engulfs, change is dependable.

—Nora Greyson's journal

January 2018

"She's dead. He shot her in the chest inside Raymond's house."

The comfort of soft fluffy down relaxed on top of my warm body that lay in the midst of peaceful tranquility. A flood of dim light gently came through the shade, and the ground was covered in the first snow of the year. He stood over me blankly. As the clock turned to 7:03 a.m., silence broke to death.

Startled by the abrupt allegation, I rolled onto my side. "She's not dead. Raymond's exaggerating. I never even heard of him owning a gun, but if he does and actually used it, he probably shot her in the foot in the worst case, Drew."

"No, Raymond isn't making this up. He's at his neighbor's house and wants us to go there. The rest of the family is on their way." Drew spoke like a stone statue, reticent and motionless.

I crawled out of bed like a mechanical doll twisted off into a twilight zone, slipped on a pair of boots and a winter coat, and discreetly exited through the back door to a quiet spot on the side of our house near a naked white birch that drooped with the weight of ice. I leaned against the siding, where I hoped not to be found, and slowly slid down in prayer. "God, if this is true, please help us."

We dropped Toby off at Leann's and drove in silence to Raymond's neighborhood. Gripping onto any idea of a possible misunderstanding, hoping this was a terrible mistake in communication, recalling the times when Falene complained about the way Seth treated Amie … But murder? That couldn't be true.

Reality crept up my spine as a daunting reaper of stolen tomorrows when I saw the yellow crime-scene tape and police cars and news reporters on Raymond's street. I stopped breathing. In eerie silence, Drew continued the drive.

The front door was cracked opened. Family members had gathered in the living room. Raymond sat in a formal arm chair accompanied by a police officer who was taking a report. Falene stared aimlessly into nowhere and nervously stroked the rhinestone collar of her hairless cat on her lap. I knelt in front of her and buried my face in her tear-drenched shirt as my subconscious survivor's guilt from years prior surfaced with a flood of untold emotions. Releasing my hold, I was suffocated by the thick, surreal reality of anger and anguish that motioned across the floor in an extraordinary sense of lost direction.

Drew sat forward in an adjacent chair with an unknowing look on his face before getting up and walking into the kitchen. "How did this happen?" he asked Uncle Carl, who was pouring a cup of coffee. "I want details. I swear I'm going to kill him."

Overhearing from the living room, Raymond stood and walked toward Drew. He removed his glasses to wipe his swollen eyes and said lugubriously, "Amie left Seth a few weeks ago, and she's been staying with me since. He was calling and texting her constantly, so she blocked him from her phone. My security camera showed her alone last night out back by the bonfire for a little while before going inside. Hours later, Seth broke in through the side window and shot her while she was sleeping. Falene and I were on our way back from a business trip when we got the call."

Falene sobbed and fumbled with a tissue in one hand with the other folded along her bony waistline as she moaned. She shook her head, covered her mouth, and buried herself in Raymond's arms.

"I heard the second gunshot while I was calling for the police," Mrs. Wilson said. "I always knew that boy was no good."

Outside the window, splatters of cruel, bright red contrasted with the pure, white snow.

Aunt Terry offered another tissue to Falene and took her hand. "Seth was stalking Amie for hours before he broke in. They have it on surveillance. He was taken by ambulance but died before reaching the hospital."

Drew walked back into the living room, sat for a brief moment, and listened to the ongoing questions from the police officer. After less than thirty minutes of our being there, he stood and announced that he needed to go home to walk our new puppy.

And then we left.

CHAPTER 31

Pink. She loved the color pink, and so the flowers were decided. Delicately displayed surrounding a cross, some tall bouquets were mixed with white lilies, greenery, and baby's breath. Some mixed with soft purple carnations. Neighboring them would sit large framed photos of Amie's pretty face.

I met with family around an oversized conference table at the funeral home to help with the arrangements. Drew had been burying himself in work pulling twelve-hour shifts six days a week and was unable to meet us there.

Mia decided on the urn and a few trinkets she would later give to close family members who requested to carry sentiments of Amie's remains.

"What did she like to do?" the funeral director asked with a pen and paper in hand.

"She loved spending time with her family," I replied. "When she wasn't working, that's what Amie would do."

As his questions continued for her obituary, his voice trailed off into a blur.

Afterward, I searched the internet for a venue, decided on the menu, and reserved the date. But it felt that it must have been for someone else.

CHAPTER 32

The service was remarkably beautiful; Amie's life was brought to light instead of swept into the darkness that had stolen it. The line of mourners trailed out the doors for hours. Many people shared deep condolences and stories about their times with Amie, but what struck me the most were the few family members of Seth's who had bravely attended to pay their respects. The poor souls seemed to be drowning in the cavernous shame of Seth's ferocious actions; they were pacing aimlessly as if they were lost children captured in the black shadows of despair with no escape. They trembled about uncontrollably repeating over and over in a helpless manner, "I'm sorry. I'm so sorry. God help us please, I'm so very sorry."

I felt such pity. I wanted to grab them and tell them it wasn't their fault. I wanted to somehow find a way to calm them down in fear that they would literally drop dead in front of us of heart attacks. They wore the burden like ten lead coats, but in truth, they had not had a single thing to do with Seth's plan to murder Amie. Not a single thing.

The days that followed were spent closely monitoring the television as Amie's murder-suicide was unfolding with newfound details and was being broadcast on every news station for weeks, which felt more like years. I stood vigilantly when Toby flipped through to find his favorite cartoons. After he wasn't in the room anymore, as much as I didn't want to see Amie's beautiful face advertised alongside Seth's and the sanguinary gruesome details that stole her life over and over again, Drew insisted on our watching.

CHAPTER 33

I notified Toby's school about our family tragedy. I was worried that he might get approached if someone connected him to the news reports by last name, and Drew and I agreed that Toby was too young to realize the truth about the way his aunt had died.

Toby had asked why he hadn't seen or talked to her. Knowing we had to at least tell him that she wasn't with us on earth anymore, we decided to say that she had died in a car accident. That made Toby sad enough as he recalled all the birthday celebrations with all our family gathering to honor his yearly milestones. Aunty Amie would always be the one to arrive first, at least twenty minutes early, and she would walk through the door with the biggest smile and the largest gift bag stuffed with presents for Toby.

She had loved her family and especially the children. She had been my sister-in-law for almost fifteen years. Never again would we share special times together or our sisterly love for each other. It was a robbery that in no way could be replaced.

CHAPTER 34

As I huddle in solitude and silence among this gravel
night, I search for a remnant of hope in darkness
that forced its sight. But my will seek the Angel of
Wisdom to dwell on sacred script, and in this place
transforms life that's stole; Thy too shall forsake me
into bitterness, but receive a hungry soul.

—Nora Greyson's journal

Go to bed at 12:30 a.m. Get up at 2:30 a.m. Get back to bed at 5:30
a.m. Rise at 7:30 a.m. and I no longer know what day of the week it
is. I know that beyond Amie's death, Drew was filled with unspoken
anger because he could no longer seek revenge on the person who
had stolen his twin sister's life.

He mostly sat quietly. Too quietly, and that made me nervous
though I didn't show it. Everyone kept asking me how he was doing,
but I really didn't know. Sometimes, I sat quietly with him. Other
times, I let him be alone. Once in a while, I tried small talk, and
occasionally, I dared to console him. I suddenly felt insufficient and
lost on how to approach my husband.

The few times Drew spoke about Amie's death, he expressed
his anger toward himself for not having protected her. I knew he
needed me, so outside of caring for Toby and attending to my work,

I'd been dedicating my time to trying to hold Drew up, which became like walking on eggshells. In addition, for thirty minutes each morning, I faithfully started my day attending to Falene's cries on my way to work, and I accept her numerous calls throughout my workday trying to comfort her. I was left with no time to grieve myself, and I became extremely exhausted but couldn't find rest or peace anywhere.

Worse yet, I knew it was just a matter of time before Drew exploded, and the anticipation of that filled my mind with visions of how my own death could have occurred in the heat of his drunken moment three years earlier. I had been watching Drew closely, and I thanked God he had not relapsed into drinking. Not up to then at least.

During dinner, Drew showed me a picture that was taken moments after Amie's death. It was a clear depiction of a devil forming from the blood spatters in the snow. It horrified me. Drew paced the floor in acts of blasphemy and verbally challenged the devil into his life claiming he would beat him for all the evil that had happened. I tried unsuccessfully to explain to Drew that it simply didn't work that way. The devil was a spirit, and you couldn't physically hit a spirit, but that seemed like too much reality for Drew to accept.

After dinner, I went into my room alone. I closed the door and in frustration, extreme exhaustion and hopelessness pleaded with God to show Himself to me in human form somehow. Looking back, that sounds like I was asking for Him to reincarnate Jesus in the flesh and bring Him to me, which my right mind knew was impossible. I suppose that showed how insane I was beginning to feel. Nevertheless, I desperately needed words directly spoken to me from a trustworthy source, and He knew this source needed to be stronger than me to rely on for guidance and rest.

PART IV

THE LIGHT IN THE DARKNESS

For by grace you have been saved through faith, and that not of yourselves; it is the gift of God, not of works, lest anyone should boast.

—Ephesians 2:8–9 (NKJV)

CHAPTER 35

February 2018

I hadn't realized yet the simple complexity of God's love and that He already loved me completely when He gave me life. I'd done nothing to earn His love, and I couldn't perceive of any way to make Him love me more. It was through faith and prayer that He granted me the gift of His grace. Not because I had ever done anything extraordinary. Nor was I for any reason more valuable to Him than anyone else was. Not anyone.

A few days earlier, I'd called a priest at our parish. I had witnessed him celebrating Mass, and I felt he presented himself as a true bellwether and a sincere adherent of God. I wanted to ask him to pray for Amie's soul along with the rest of us left behind and devastated. It was my plan to only have a one-time encounter, but it was God's plan to give me an unexpected gift of the deepest spiritual friendship that excelled way beyond my imagination.

Our first conversation took place over the phone. When Fr. Ebuka asked me the reason for my call, I briefly described Amie's death and the distraught state of our family. After a moment of silence, he offered his condolences and prayers and then gently asked me to meet with him in his office. If ever a life-changing moment could be identified with gratitude for the grace of God and His mercy that was certainly it for me.

CHAPTER 36

The sun was bright upon the white-covered evergreens as gusts of wind rustled the snow loose and caused it to glitter like silver dust in front of the rectory. I spotted Fr. Ebuka slowly treading the grounds near the entry while praying adjacent to the statue of the Blessed Virgin Mary. Not wanting to disturb him and thinking he had no idea who I was, I walked past him and went into the rectory. His secretary escorted me to his office that was beautifully decorated with dark mahogany wainscot and lustrous cherry furniture.

"Father requested to be immediately informed upon your arrival." She left to summon him closing the door behind her. Never having had this experience before, I felt a boost of importance that a spiritual leader would make such a request on my behalf, but that feeling quickly changed to anxiety as I considered my emotional state and worried that I might do or say something offensive in front of the priest.

When Fr. Ebuka entered and sat in the chair next to me instead of at the large, intimidating desk in front of me, I felt at ease. He remained imperturbable as he asked me to repeat the story. He patiently listened to me. It seemed that he was somehow able to naturally experience the same pain I was experiencing while becoming an additional source of calm and comfort in the room as I slowly relived the details.

Father's hundred-year-old soul relaxed in his oversized upholstered chair. His head slightly lowered before he gently said, "It's okay to cry."

"Okay, Father," I replied and sat for a moment trying to gain a sense of self. Tears slowly streamed from my eyes and then turned into sobs as my hands met my face for solace. I remained until I felt the relief momentarily complete.

I looked up. He hadn't changed his position—physically, emotionally, or spiritually.

"Father, I know the importance of forgiveness, and I'm trying to understand how to do this."

"You are really inspiring me," he said.

How humbled I felt to hear that from a priest. After all, I was just a regular person. Soon after I appreciated his acknowledgement, I realized how long it had been since my emotional well-being felt any more validated than a quarter-page of a scribbled line lost in the past of an old, dusty book. Somewhere along the sands of time, I had gone from human to robot.

"You must keep forgiving," he said.

Before that moment, I hadn't realized that forgiveness was something people needed to keep doing to restore peace in their lives, and I wondered if I could do this indefinitely.

Other than a few kind words and the recommendation of two books about forgiveness—*Left to Tell* by Immaculee Ilibagiza and *Nurturing Healing Love* by Scarlett Lewis—he didn't speak much, and it was a great relief for me to feel heard in this peaceful setting.

I asked him if I could share a picture with him but said that I wasn't sure if it was appropriate.

Maintaining his equanimity, he replied, "Well, it's only a picture."

"Yes, but it's not a good one."

"How bad could it really be when in fact it's only a picture?"

I took a deep breath and slowly brought up the photo that had been taken just a few hours after Amie was murdered, the photo Drew had shared with me that depicted an image of a devil from the splattered blood in the snow outside of Raymond's window, with a clearly identifiable face, shoulders, horns, and stance that included him holding a pitchfork.

Fr. Ebuka looked at the picture carefully. "This is a good picture because the devil is behind the cross. He is afraid of the cross and will never come before it. Focus on the cross," he said before handing me back my cell phone.

The image of the devil was so pronounced and so startling that I hadn't noticed the position of the two pieces of wood portraying a definite shape of a cross laying on top the devil image as if the cross was forcing the devil to stay back. It almost looked as though the cross was in its perfect form supernaturally.

From that point on, whether knowingly or unknowingly, Father brought me closer to God, right where I needed to be.

Once we finished talking, he stood and offered his hands. I stood facing him. As he prayed, the Holy Spirit emanated through his words, and I listened attentively as he asked God with pure confidence to ease my pain. After his eyes opened, he asked me to see him again soon. I was surprised but glad for his request.

He offered his cell phone number in case I needed him between meetings, which for some reason seemed strange to me. I supposed I hadn't thought a priest would own a cell phone. After all, he was a holy man of significant importance. How else would he have kept up with essential calls? Maybe I was expecting him to have an ancient telegram device reserved for only the most pious.

While driving home, I was astonished at the tremendous relief I felt after having spent only a few hours with Fr. Ebuka, as if he had already prepared to be my spiritual caretaker. I supposed that was one of the duties of a priest. I guessed I just had never thought about it before, nor have I ever experienced such intense compassion. I became filled with gratitude realizing this was not just serendipity but God answering my prayers. I immediately looked forward to sharing the encouragement with Drew and to my next meeting with Fr. Ebuka.

CHAPTER 37

I read both books Father had suggested and was intrigued by the courage, strength, and spiritual evolvement of these survivors both having risen from horrific circumstances. Their lessons were implied, and I appreciated this new insight.

We spoke more deeply about forgiveness. In recognizing my growth, Father openly prayed for all that was lost and all that was left behind. Today, just like the end of the last meeting, I was amazed at how good I felt after leaving his presence.

Each time we met, I entered his office with the thought *There's no way he's going to make me feel better today*, but a few short hours later, I would walk away feeling like a new person floating as light as a feather. At some point, it almost become like a challenge that I would always thankfully fail. I soon became fascinated and curious about my new priest friend's captivating eloquence and capability for restoration, so I did some research. What I discovered grounded me to my seat with admiration. This was no ordinary priest.

Fr. Ebuka had started his journey toward priesthood during early adolescence with minor seminary training and then major seminary training followed by two bachelors' degrees. He was chosen out of hundreds in his class to continue studies overseas, where he achieved three masters' degrees and a MBBS which is considered to be the equivalent of an MD in the United States.

CHAPTER 38

"People do not care how much you know, until they know how much you care."

—Fr. Ebuka

"I researched your name. Thank you for not telling me about all your extensive education and your medical degree. If I had known, I might have been too intimidated to reach out to you," I told him.

Father sat calmly, put his hand in the air, and shook his head. "Don't worry about my education. It doesn't mean anything. I didn't educate myself to become vertical with myself. I educated myself to become horizontal with people."

In reverence and awe, I sat speechless and filled with deep gratitude that God had given me him.

Realizing the extraordinary impact Fr. Ebuka was having on my life, I asked Drew if he would also meet with him, but he refused. Knowing he desperately needed help, I gently suggested other forms of counseling, but much to my disappointment, he refused that too. So instead, I periodically shared some good advice that I'd learned through my meetings with Fr. Ebuka, and Drew seemed to be opened to that at least a little bit.

Cocooned in dense fog, we slowly made footprints down the snow-covered trail that led to an old oak tree behind their childhood home where Drew and Amie used to play when they were children. He held her remains close to his chest as if trying to hug her one last time. The air was heavy and still except for our frozen breaths that barely escaped us.

Silently, Drew removed the top of the urn and began to spread Amie's ashes around the ground below a worn tire swing that hung like a lonely lost soul. His eyes settled toward a painted sign nailed to the trunk. He approached and laid his hand over the aged but bold dark blue letters: **ANDREW AND AMIE PLAY HERE— KEEP OUT!**

I bowed and recited a prayer hoping that might bring Drew some sense of comfort. No other words were spoken. As flurries turned into rain, we watched the last of Amie's remains wash into the earth. In deep sorrow, we said our final goodbyes before turning back. She would be forever loved and forever missed.

CHAPTER 39

Eternal echoes reap the sound of grief in heavy hearts, and I will not forgive a killer of life and allow him to win any right.

—Nora Greyson's journal

"Father, I feel so angry, and I want you to take back that prayer you said from our last meeting. I changed my mind. I don't want to forgive Seth," I said.

Leaning forward, he slapped his desk and firmly chastised. "I will not take back that prayer. I know what I'm talking about. You're going to ruin your relationship with your husband and your whole life. You must forgive!"

I sprung into a stand and told Father I wasn't feeling well and wanted to leave.

"You don't have to leave," he replied.

"I want to. I'm done with this meeting for today. I'm sorry." I left.

CHAPTER 40

The lesson of the single egg.

—Nora Greyson's journal

"I'm glad you came back. We had a rough week last week, but I think we're still moving forward," Father assured me as his thin frame leaned over a small dish that held a single hard-boiled egg. He made the sign of the cross and with a grateful smile, he blessed his one-egg meal and offered me half, which I couldn't conceive of accepting. "How are you?" he asked sincerely.

I was relieved by that question. *Most people have stopped asking me that*, I thought miserably. "I'm sorry, Father, for asking you to take back the prayer from our previous meeting. It's just that Seth killed Amie because he felt that if he couldn't have her, nobody should. I think he thought that by killing her and then himself, they'd be together forever. I feel like my forgiving him allows that to happen."

"I see the confusion now, but that's not true. Heaven is a state of being, not a geographical location." He looked exceptionally peaceful. "When we die with our sins forgiven, we are right in front of God's face."

CHAPTER 41

After great loss are the remnants of love with no place to go. It's time to give it away—to find something bigger than myself to spend love on.

—Nora Greyson's journal

"How are you today?" Father asked. "And how's your family?"

"We're trying our best. I appreciate your asking. Father, I've been thinking about your mission. I'm interested in knowing more about it. Would you share some details with me?"

"I didn't know you'd want to do that." He seemed surprised and pleased. "Well, the group is having a meeting this afternoon. If you'd like to join us, you're welcome to. They'll be talking about upcoming fundraisers to support the building of a hospital in my hometown in Nigeria. Nora, there are different types of love in this world. Spiritual love is the strongest, and emotional love comes in second. I have seen it become very beneficial for people to be involved in a charity, but it doesn't necessarily have to be mine. There are a lot of good charities out there and plenty of people who need prayers and emotional support."

But I'd already made up my mind, and a few hours later, I was in a room being introduced to some amazing people. I wondered why they all seemed to be so pleasantly joyful. Maybe they realized a deeper, spiritually satisfied life, or maybe I'd been consumed by so much misery that I'd forgotten what it was like to be around anything else. Either way, I was hungry, and it wasn't long before I desired to be like them.

CHAPTER 42

More than 20 million children live in a home without the physical presence of a father. Millions more have dads who are physically present, but emotionally absent. If it were classified as a disease, fatherlessness would be an epidemic worthy of attention as a national emergency.

—National Center for Fathering

Sitting by dim window light, I watched reruns of the news reports on Amie's death over and over, rewind and replay, rewind and replay. There was an interview with Seth Kruiger's father. I couldn't tell if his eyes were full of shame, guilt or indifference when he said he hasn't been in contact with his son in over thirty years, but there was something about his proclamation that set my curiosity on fire and I began researching the topic of fatherlessness.

What I discovered about growing up without a father was alarming. Research showed the effects of fatherlessness on children comprise of low self-esteem, feelings of being damaged and unwanted, a constant psychological search for a reason their fathers had left them and moments of self-loathing. Guilt develops through an infestation of depression influenced by a flawed thought process that the child had done something wrong to cause the abandonment or could have done something to prevent it. In many cases, this sense of disconnection evolved into a loss of identity for the child.

Ben Spencer wrote in the *Daily Mail*, "Growing up without a father could permanently alter the structure of the brain." Of all the information I had taken in so far, that was the most disturbing.

Reports indicated that fatherless children were more likely to do poorly in school and over 70 percent were high school dropouts. As they reached adulthood and throughout it they experienced difficulty holding on to employment, settle for low-paying jobs and depend on social assistance; many end up homeless.

Internalizing from an incredible amount of emptiness and fear, fatherless children are likely to develop side effects such as anger, grief, fatigue, anxiety, low self-esteem, panic attacks, clinginess, sleeping and eating disorders, lack of energy, lack of creativity, lack of motivation, lack of capacity to adjust socially, asthma, digestive disorders, chronic headaches, and through a desperate need to fill the void, a vulnerability forms that often guides them to become attracted to negative influences pushing many into lifestyles of substance abuse who are easily targeted by sex offenders.

Many of these children are consumed with quiet anger born from the pain of rejection that manifests in toxic shame and then develops into a debilitating false belief that they are not good enough to be valued. This intensifies when rejection is repeated in adulthood through other relationships.

Children who understand that it isn't acceptable to misbehave in public hold their quiet anger inside, where it insidiously builds over time inside their fiercely protected solitary confinement of incapacitating emotions. This isolated self-imprisonment paralyzes their capability to have a flexible psychological response system resulting in stunted emotional growth that suffocates their innate goodness and leaves them with the false impression that their behavior problems should somehow be self-controlled. Unless validation of feelings occurs and anger finds a proper release, they will eventually burst with demoralizing results. This explains why fatherless children and especially boys are twice as likely to end up in prison, and almost 65 percent of fatherless children have attempted suicide.

Research has shown that not meeting children's emotional needs can confirm to the children that they must be defective, and that could lead to the lack of ability to distinguish right from wrong. Extreme passiveness has occurred as a result of neglect in paternal love especially with girls who attempt to compensate their loss egocentrically as a rejection of their fathers by devaluing themselves as they seek to find acceptance from males by becoming sexually active in early adolescence causing a rapid rise in the number of single teenage mothers with less than a high school degree.

On the other side of the spectrum, fatherless children can be very aggressive. They often feel a need to be dominating in relationships and are prone to violent behavior when their sense of control is threatened as they become determined to prove they're in nondisposable at any cost, resulting in a one hundred times higher risk of fatal abuse.

> According to 72.2% of the U.S. population, fatherlessness is the most significant family or social problem facing America. —National Center for Fathering, Fathering in America Poll, January, 1999.

Emotionally absent fathers who have been separated from their children usually by divorce are highly prone to neglecting and even discarding their children who vertically represent their mothers in physical appearance, and the outcome is almost equally devastating regardless of the father's best efforts to be supportive financially and in physical presence.

America has one of the highest levels of single-parent families with children in the world. About 30 percent of America's families with children under 18 years old, amounting to 10 million households, are single-parent families, a tripled number since 1965. —the hill.com, March 19, 2021

I wondered why approximately 30 percent of reported children in America were living in single parent homes but this subject wasn't found to be getting much attention. It seems to have become the blind-eyed devastating trend that when we allow ourselves to think about it, we feel momentarily sympathetic for those who live with it, but then we shake it off and move on with our lives, however consequently this problem affects the total population. There is a much greater chance that fatherless children will have fatherless children or at least pass their aggressiveness and emotional disregard to their next generation.

When tracing back the pattern of fatherlessness, I discovered that according to past statistics starting in 1970, we can project an average increase of approximately 7.89 percent per future decade over the next thirty years. I can only assume this means by the year 2050, the number of children living in single-parent households may increase to approximately 2,500,000.

> It's easier to build strong children than to repair broken men.
> —Frederick Douglass

As I became more engrossed in this topic, I tried to reach out to community programs that included an idea of the awareness of fatherlessness only to receive empathetic lip service along with the excuse that there just wasn't sufficient funding to do anything about this epidemic or more truthfully put, it wasn't a financial priority regardless of the copious information available on the consequences of fatherlessness. My overwhelming frustrations compiled into what felt like a completely hopeless cry out that landed on deaf ears of those who were undermining the root of one of the most destructive family crisis of our creation.

CHAPTER 43

May 2018

The unpredictable New England weather went from winter directly into summer with no spring. The day was hot and humid as I tapped my hands on the steering wheel to the music coming from my car radio. I approached a red light, and to my right, I saw on a piece of cardboard, **"Please help. God bless."**

He stood in the scorching heat on top of black pavement in a parking lot. It was rare to see a homeless person in this town. Begging a second glance, he struck me as odd because he looked much too young to be standing alone at an intersection. I rolled down my window and yelled, "Hey, are you okay?"

"Yes," he replied.

"How old are you?"

"Thirty-three."

I was surprised because he looked barely fifteen. I searched my wallet, but since I hadn't been to the bank yet, I didn't have a single dollar on me, and since I hadn't purchased groceries yet, I had no food to offer. "Take care of yourself," I said feeling sorry for him. Words were literally all I was able to give.

I drove away with an awful nagging sense. I kept driving ahead on the main road until I arrived at the store, where I purchased a foot-long grinder, chips, and large bottled water leaving my personal list for later. I drove back to the spot where the homeless man had been only to find him gone. I decided to drive farther down the road hoping to locate him along the way, and I did. He was about to enter a liquor store when I pulled into the parking lot and yelled to him. I parked in an open area where there was a clear view of the road, and I walked toward him. As he met my approach, I asked if he believed in God not knowing where in the world my words were coming from or what I was doing there.

"I think I'm even with God now," he replied rebelliously.

I didn't ask him what he meant by that. "Could I pray for you?" I asked still unsure of what I was doing.

"Yes."

"What's your name?"

"Jonathan. My father just passed away, and as of yesterday, I'm a new father myself."

I allowed a moment without interruption.

"Would you mind praying for my mother too? Her name's Dalia."

It felt like something outside of me took over. "What's your child's name?"

"Max."

We stood in broad daylight in the parking lot between a liquor store and a busy street. I extended my hands to this homeless stranger. I asked God to please bring hope into his life, provide him with a job, and watch over his mother, Dalia. When I finished, I opened my eyes only to see his still closed. His hands were still holding mine as if they were a lifesaver thrown across rough seas. My thoughts flashed back to my recent research on fatherlessness, and I found myself speaking to him about the importance of being a good dad.

"I was brought to you for a reason," I started as he slowly opened his eyes. I placed my hands on his shoulders while looking at him. "I'm supposed to let you know that you're important. In fact, you're very important, and your son needs you." I spoke even though I still had no idea where my words were coming from, but the message flowed.

Without moving an inch, he thanked me.

I turned to retrieve the food I'd purchased for him from my vehicle along with a few dollars I had stowed in the bag clearly knowing the risk of his buying liquor with it, but I wasn't there to judge. After handing him the goods, I drove away.

Maybe it happened because of my recent state of subliminal humility, or maybe it was God working through me. Either way, I had never done anything like that. Rather than feeling awkward as it seemed I should have since this was so uncharacteristic of me, quite the opposite occurred. It was more like a state of spiritual euphoria or perhaps religious ecstasy. Logically speaking, I realized I had put myself at risk of a potentially dangerous situation, but when I drove away, I knew that what I had done was barely of my own doing anyway, and my ordinary day had become an extraordinary gift, one that I will never forget.

To my disappointment, as I shared this story with Drew, his only reply was, "If I can get a job, so could he."

CHAPTER 44

An angry man's heart is held captive by his mistress of sorrow.

—Nora Greyson's journal

In our dimly lit bedroom, Drew lay quietly all day. I was relieved that he was mourning, but I'd never seen him so depressed. He had been keeping this all inside, but then, it was flowing like a river into a deep sea of unspoken sadness.

He acted so loving toward me at times yet at other times so withdrawn. I lay beside him and let nothing else matter but this. We rest and remain bleak into the night. The tension Drew had pooled inside led me to a strong sense that things were about to go bad. I couldn't sleep.

Around 5:00 a.m., Drew got ready for work. He hugged and kissed me as he always did and then left. In silence, I prayed to the Blessed Mother for sempiternal protection. Toward the end of praying, I pictured her appearing over me. She placed her hand on my chest and then disappeared. I am quite aware that sometimes we want things so badly that we can create visions of them.

CHAPTER 45

My back was against the church wall during the receiving line. I was trying to catch my breath before facing him. The deacon noticed and took my hand trying to assure me that everything was going to be okay.

The announcement came at the end of Mass, and I swallowed tightly afraid I might get sick in the pew. Fr. Ebuka was being transferred to a parish outside of town. Although I'd known all along about the risk of starting counseling with a priest, I hadn't expected for his transfer to happen so shortly after our beginning to meet. After all, he had been at our parish for two months.

"My dear, remember I told you that I had something important to talk to you about. I'm sorry this is happening right in the middle of your healing process," Fr. Ebuka said sincerely.

"How long have you known?" My voice was shaking.

"I just found out a few days ago. We'll talk soon."

Still in shock, I held my gaze with my lips pressed shut tightly before I was able to finally speak. "Okay, Father."

I looked down, left the church, and drove home despondently.

CHAPTER 46

Several women were working in the kitchen preparing and distributing the food people had brought for the farewell party. The hall was packed with parishioners some to receive last-minute advice, some for special blessings, but all to wish him the best on his journey to his new location. It amazed me how many people became so close to him in such a short period of time. The line circled around the church hall. Toby was anxiously but patiently waiting his turn. I felt the reality of losing my source of consolation. A gentle woman placed her hand on my shoulder to assure me that things would be okay. I hadn't noticed, but I must have been wearing my emotions on my sleeve. I was glad for her kindness.

After most of the crowd left, Father approached and offered his gratitude for our attendance. He asked where Drew was, hoping to finally meet him, but Drew was still recovering from his bout of depression the previous day had left him with.

CHAPTER 47

July 2018

In Nigeria

Their restless cries will be heard, and the longing, wide-eyed orphans will gather. His flight will bring deliverance and comfort and rest, and the hospital plans will be managed as honest as a bluebird sits to protect her nest. So too shall the foundation prepare for its mighty structure of salvation.

And then all will come and watch in satiated joy. And aside his sublime virtue they will worship and rejoice and sing and dance and eat. But he will hold no sanctimonious. To God be all the glory!

Nevermore will her paper-thin skin bear a single tear, and the innocent will thrive in understanding.

In Rhode Island

People were scattered about in pandemonium as time drew near. Some gossiped in confusion while others sat firmly planted. The hall was crowded with anticipation and aspiration that the vicar's appearance would relieve them from chaotic propaganda. A few of us who knew Fr. Ebuka well hoped the truth would be revealed.

The vicar began cautiously approaching this sensitive issue. As each of us took turns standing at the podium, emotions took their peak in distress.

Parishioner 1: "We don't understand what's going on. We had a great priest who was abruptly removed without any explanation. Now we don't have a priest at all."

Parishioner 2: "By asking for donations to support his mission in Nigeria, it's taking away from people donating to our Catholic school. That is something we simply cannot afford."

Parishioner 3: "Isn't being charitable to the poor and helping widows and orphans in their distress a major part of being a Christian?"

Parishioner 4: "In my opinion, the only reason Fr. Ebuka isn't pastor is because he wasn't ordained in the US."

Parishioner 5: "Why has Fr. Ebuka been transferred so much? How could a priest possibly accomplish anything when he's constantly being moved?"

Parishioner 6: "It is so disappointing to know the careless and unjust way this transfer was handled. If someone would just be honest, maybe we can start to forgive the way Christian's are supposed to."

Our parish has become divided, and in this schism, people were choosing sides. I sat in disbelief. Do we not see many priests in other parishes asking for support for overseas ministries? Some of our locals were acting like this was a forbidden and absurd request that no priest had ever made before, while many others showed their strong disapproval of the heedless manner of Fr Ebuka's transfer as vacillating talk continued to steal the air.

· The pressured vicar ended the meeting by telling us that we would receive answers to many of our questions in a few weeks, but apparently, due to the tremendous amount of emphasis on exculpating Fr. Ebuka, instead of waiting a few weeks, we had a speaker return in a few days.

In the end Fr. Ebuka was right. The meeting made no difference concerning his outcome.

PART V

THE MERCURIAL DEBACLE RESURFACED

There's only one true way to know a person's future—that is to look at his or her past. A repeated mistake isn't any more a mistake than an apology could be valid without change. This instead is manipulation.

—Nora Greyson's journal

CHAPTER 48

I entered my house to the unpleasant mess Olive, our dog, had made on our living room floor. It had clearly been stepped in, tracked, and left uncleaned. I knew right away there was something wrong because Drew would never have left the house in that condition.

He and Toby were at the grocery store for some last-minute items for a Labor Day barbecue with Raymond and Falene. Drew hadn't called me all day. That was very unusual. Even more so, he hadn't responded to any of my messages.

When Drew and Toby returned, I could tell that the day was going to be *that* day—that dark, dreaded, sinister day I knew was inevitable. I was still cleaning the floor when they walked through the door. I did not let Drew see my concern; I greeted him with a usual kiss. The arrogance of his complacent demeanor confirmed he had been drinking.

Toby was older, and he was in our presence. It was way too early in the day for me to send him to bed. I had to ride this out as calmly as possible. Regardless of my attempt to act sanguine, Drew was very agitated even though I barely spoke. As we ate dinner, he continuously dropped his utensils and his food.

"Is something wrong with Drew?" I whispered to Raymond after Drew left the table.

"He seems fine to me," he replied.

When Drew returned, his breath reeked of alcohol. He stumbled as he sat back down.

"Are you okay?" I asked him.

"How dare you ask that? You don't appreciate anything!" Drew firmly spoke in a derogatory way as he attempted to stand.

The volatile relapse started in almost the same way it had three years earlier. I stood slowly and walked away.

Drew stood and followed me. "Get in the bathroom!" he demanded grabbing my arm. He shut and locked the door behind us. "You undeserving, worthless woman! Are you accusing me of drinking?" He was staring me down.

I stared back but said nothing.

"You better not ever ask me that again!" he remarked punitively even though I had never mentioned anything about drinking. His putrid breath almost caused my skin to turn green as I tried to hold mine while waiting for him to break his ominous glare.

Finally, he opened the bathroom door. I walked out. My eyes burned as I fought back tears of abhorrence because I knew what was about to unfold.

Falene sat watching Toby play outside with some neighborhood friends. I was glad for the distraction. Trying to avoid Drew, I kept a distance, but he followed me like a probe repetitively shaming me and accusing me of questioning his drinking. I escaped momentarily and sat at the edge of my bed with my hand over my mouth. *God, help me,* I squeezed my eyes in request and then hurried back for the fear of what might happen if I stayed out of sight for too long.

Cleaning the table, I spotted Drew making a bonfire.

"I want s'mores!" Toby said with excitement.

"I'm kinda tired tonight, Toby," I said. "Maybe we could do this tomorrow instead."

Drew's gaze was intimidating. I sat without reaction.

Resting my head on the patio chair, I watched Drew independently grow angrier in his own mind. Out from the silence, he began yelling, cussing, and threatening me as Falene, Toby, and a few neighborhood children stood by stunned and confused.

"Go home now," I told the children. I looked Drew straight in the eye and with all my heart I told him I loved him and to please calm down.

"I don't want to hear it!" he screamed.

Toby started crying. "Daddy, stop! Daddy, please stop!"

But Drew was unresponsive to his son's plea. Toby walked with his bicycle over to his father and placed his hand over his dad's mouth and tearfully said, "Daddy, please, what did Mommy ever do to you? What did she do to deserve this, Daddy?"

"Look at Toby, Drew," Raymond demanded, but Drew's eyes remained malevolent preparing to attack and take me under.

I stood and walked toward the house. Drew followed and stopped me in the doorway. His temper got worse. I turned around and calmly placed my hand on his arm "Drew, I'm your wife, and I love you. I'm here for you."

"Don't touch me!" Drew shouted and shrugged my hand off. "My sister was murdered, and you want me to calm *down?*"

Toby stood right behind his dad and heard the truth about his aunt's death for the first time in that way. Falene and I stood silently in shock, and I knew Drew was about to completely lose it.

Toby was sobbing and trembling. I took him by the hand and brought him close to me.

"Knock it off, Drew," Raymond said and ordered him to sit down outside.

I brought Toby inside. Drew was not himself, and after what had transpired three years earlier, I was no stranger to whom he was about to become. This time Toby would witness everything. With that fear in mind, I called 911 knowing that as long as Drew obeyed the police, he would not be arrested because he hadn't physically done anything to me or threatened my life. It was a fifty-fifty chance, but waiting for anything else to happen was not an option, and I knew I could keep Toby inside if things became messy outside.

I just needed the police to safely remove Drew from us and away from our home for the night.

"We were called about a disturbance," I heard an officer speak from outside my bedroom window. Another officer entered our house and questioned me about the call. Drew remained calm. Meanwhile, Toby became hysterical at the sight of the police.

"Falene, come and comfort Toby so I can speak to the officer privately," I asked.

"I'm going to throw up! I can't breathe!" Toby fretfully paced. "Please don't take my daddy to jail! My daddy's nice and didn't do anything wrong." As he pleaded, my heart shattered and my anger toward Drew emerged from an old, resentful spirit.

"He's willing to leave for the night," an officer told me. Raymond took Drew's keys to drive them back to his house, where he would presumably stay. Drew's fierce eyes recessed deep into his skull, and when they locked on mine, I saw pure hate.

They left. With my back up against the closed front door, I slowly exhaled. The next day marked eight months since Amie's death.

"Olive, come inside." I called out, but she skittishly dodged my approach and hid under our hydrangea bush. "Come on, pup," I called out and then bent down to pick her up. As I held Olive, her shiny black, puppy fur body trembled in my arms. I sighed. Dogs never lied.

Back inside, I secured every window and door. After long hours of calming Toby down and finally getting him to sleep, I sat alone feeling consumed by defeat. I was terrified that Drew was going to come back. He had a car and was full of booze and vengeance. I thought about taking Toby and going into protective hiding where no one would ever find us, but I knew I'd be forbidden to have any outside contact once I made that move. But the plan I'd set in place three years before still existed, and if forced to run, I would.

During times like that, anger should be separated from its typical bad reputation because it promoted the fight-or-flight response essential for survival. It is my God-given right to allow my anger to heighten my focus and remove all obstacles in the way of safety for a clear view of what is attainable instead of fearing what seems impossible.

He who has a why to live can bear almost any how.
—Friedrich Nietzsche

CHAPTER 49

"I can't believe he did that to you. He wouldn't let up. He was so persistent. I don't know what to say. I can't believe he acted that way," Falene said.

I was glad she had witnessed Drew's behavior that time.

"I'm going to stop by and pick up my clothes for work, but I'm not staying. I need some time to myself. I can't believe you called the police," Drew said.

He was still angry, but I wasn't afraid because that day, he was sober.

His mood was cold when he arrived the next day for his belongings. We barely spoke.

Bending down to Toby, he said, "Toby, I love you, but I'm having a hard time dealing with Aunty Amie's death. I need a little time to myself. I'll be staying at Raymond and Falene's."

Clinging to Drew's neck, Toby said, "I love you, Daddy. I'm going to miss you. When will you be back?"

"Let's see how I feel next week, okay? Don't forget how much I love you. I'll call you tonight."

Drew left without saying a single word to me.

CHAPTER 50

He shall cover you with His feathers, and under
His wings you shall take refuge; His truth shall be
your shield and buckler. You shall not be afraid of
the terror by night, Nor of the arrow that flies by
day, Nor of the pestilence that walks in darkness,
Nor of the destruction that lays waste at noonday.
A thousand may fall at your side, and ten thousand
at your right hand; but it shall not come near you.
(Psalm 91:4–7 NKJV)

Dear God, I'm so worried about my marriage and about what Toby
witnessed the other night. How is he processing all this? There's
no good way to explain to an eight-year-old that his aunt had been
murdered by a man who used to bring him toys and go fishing with
him and that his father has flipped out because of it.

An antique-looking book sat on a shelf: *The Romance of Tristram
and Iseult*. It has sat there for years never read. For some reason,
I took it down and fanned through it until my thumb suddenly
stopped. At a glance, I saw the word *God*. The section read,

"Friend, may God protect you! The King is wrong
to hate you. But whithersoever you go, God will be

your true friend." She fled and came to her chamber, where Bragwaine received her, trembling, in her arms: the Queen related the adventure. Bragwaine exclaimed: "Iseult, my lady, God has wrought a great miracle for you. He is our compassionate Father, and turns away evil from those He knows to be innocent."

—Joseph Bedier

I cannot even begin to explain the feeling that came over me after reading these words. God's omniscience assured me not to fear a single thing. Suddenly smiling with confidence, I got up and left my room, and I felt very loved.

I cooked Toby a big, juicy hamburger for lunch, and he also had a banana, blueberry, peanut butter, and chocolate milkshake. Just before we finished, there was a knock at our front door. Leann stood holding a baby chick.

We ventured off to her farm, and Toby brought his bicycle. He chased the chickens, and they chased him. He fed the cows and biked the trail around the pond and through the fields. And I relaxed on her front porch with a glass of iced tea feeling glad to be with her.

CHAPTER 51

"Hi, Mommy!" Toby came running to greet me at the end of his school day.

I rustled his auburn locks. "Grab your things, and let's go home to cook dinner."

As we drove away, Toby said, "Guess what, Mommy?"

"What?" I asked smiling.

"My teacher wanted us to write about what we did over the weekend in our journal, but I didn't *dooo iiiiiit*," he said proudly.

God, please help me, I prayed. Before school that morning, I had told Toby not to talk about what had happened over the weekend to anyone in fear that he would become an outcast among his classmates. Toby needed and absolutely deserved to be able to speak to a trusted adult.

"Oh, Toby, I'm so sorry. I should have spoken to you more clearly. There are a few adults in your school who are okay to talk to. Would you like to share your weekend story with them?" I asked compassionately.

"Yes, Mommy."

The following morning, I called the school counselor, who promised to visit Toby on a break from class. I sighed in relief, but I still felt bad for having misled Toby.

"Mommy, did you ever kill anyone in a car accident?" Toby asked me over dinner.

"No. Why would you ask?"

"That day Daddy was mad at you, before you came home from work, he told me he thinks the person who caused the car accident that killed Aunty Amie did it on purpose. Daddy was so mad at you. I think he thinks you caused Aunty Amie's car accident."

In a way, I was relieved that Toby hadn't derailed from the car accident story especially considering his father's inappropriate burst of brutal facts during his last episode.

As devastating as the truth was, the guilt piled on my conscience as I was stuck between telling Toby the reality or sparing his young mind from horrifying information. As the knowledge had been perceived so far, I think his mental process had evolved as expected.

CHAPTER 52

When the cause of a solution is born of a moral genius, hope prevails.

—Nora Greyson's journal

Ding. My cell phone chimed shortly after I woke in the morning. It was a video message. I walked Olive, poured my coffee, and then we both sat to watch.

On top of heart-wrenching ground, they set up large tents where sandy earth and palm trees stood in the heat of a relentless sun. The horizon displayed a devious gloat of denied resources in a discarded village overflowing with the blind and sick. People of skin and bone bent in form as they wait their turn for long overdue medical attention.

Alongside a medical doctor, six other US parishioners had traveled to Nigeria with Fr. Ebuka to provide support at a makeshift medical station. They worked tirelessly through a week-long mission as innocent victims of an unjust political system continued to arrive in search of hope.

Hundreds received free eyeglasses, and hundreds more received medical and pharmaceutical care. Young widows were trained in various marketable trades, and some were awarded grants. With their new empowerment, they were able to create self-sufficient small businesses and provide for their children. The burdens of the aging and weak widows were transposed after they accepted funds for survival, and all received at least some dignity as their expressions of gratitude testified to in the highlight of the clip.

Oppressed natives gathered closely to grasp articles of clothing being tossed their way, and at once, their faces illuminated. Children smiled joyfully as their bare toes danced on dusty ground and their arms stretched up high into blossoms of thankful hands.

Parentless babies were held, toddlers were fed, and love was spread everywhere.

One by one, Fr. Ebuka along with local priests dropped their first scoop of concrete into the ground for the beginning of the hospital's foundation, and I smiled.

To God be all the glory!

"A father of the fatherless, a defender of widows, is God in His holy habitation." (Psalm 68:5 NKJV)

CHAPTER 53

Human beings are works in progress that mistakenly think they're finished.

—Daniel Gilbert

"I know this is very difficult for you, and I'm sure you don't want to hear it, but you're going to have to find a way to forgive Seth. It took three months for me to work at feeling this much forgiveness, and I'm very aware it may take a lifetime to keep doing it, but I'm closer than I was yesterday, and that's what counts. Forgive for yourself, Drew, so you can come back to yourself and to your son free from the slavery of abhorrence.

"My thoughts become consumed with anger sometimes too. When it gets the best of me, I have to stop and question how much I have really forgiven. And then I remember that I promised myself to not allow destructive anger ruin my life and infect the people I love. And then I do whatever I can to create more-pleasant thoughts. I've come to realize that every time I resist responding to anger in a negative way, I'm rewiring my brain to obtain a greater sense of self-control."

I spoke compassionately as I struggled to find the right words and then held my breath while I waited for his response. To my surprise, Drew didn't sound angry. Though his words were of anger, his tone was sad.

"Drew, I know sometimes anger can appear to be an only remaining source of control when the devastations of our lives are out of our control eliminating at least a momentary sense of helplessness. When this happens, especially when it happens repeatedly, we can develop a tendency to become obsessed with the power of anger particularly because it's so effective in blocking other painful emotions. But at some point, we have to ask ourselves how much control do we really have especially when we begin to live in anger and it mistakenly becomes the very thing we're trying to escape, which is an additional debilitating, controlling force. It's almost like being in a constant state of offense, which causes division even from those who had nothing to do with provoking the anger. Do you think that's what's happening to you?"

"I don't know. I can't think about all that right now. I love you, I miss you, and I hate being without you."

I thought my efforts had overwhelmed him.

CHAPTER 54

Art washes away from the soul the dust of everyday life.

—Pablo Picasso

The sound of silence welcomed me to have a meeting with myself. I sat at my bench appreciating the tranquility of the soft rain as my pencil glided smoothly across a drawing pad. Toby was at school, and it was my day off work. Any remaining happiness seemed to be draining out of me lately.

Drew still texted several times a day to tell me he loved me, but I couldn't have him back here. I didn't feel safe. Whenever I told him that, he would reply "Yep" as if my concern was practically meaningless to him. I remembered a time when he couldn't stand to be more than two feet from me. It wasn't long ago that if he ever thought he had upset me, he would refuse to eat until I would forgive him even if it was over the slightest disagreement. It was almost annoying back then to have to give him so much of my reassurance and attention as if he truly depended on it.

Somewhere along the line, I accepted it, and then I kind of depended on it to feel a boost of self-importance. But it seemed that he had stopped caring if I was even alive, and I missed that old attention—sometimes. Leann once asked me if in turn I had become emotionally codependent on his dependent behavior. She was probably right that I had. *God, if Drew's having an affair, please tell me.*

I thought about divorce again, and at the time, it felt like that was what we should do. Drew had brought it up a few days earlier. He asked me if that was what I wanted, but we agreed that it was a bad time to make such a drastic decision. My heart reminded me that the 7,300 days of mostly all happiness we'd shared shouldn't be erased because of a few bad ones in between. But my mind knew that the pattern had begun again and was going to get only worse. All of his "I love you" messages had worn my judgmental aptitude thin.

I leaned back for a moment. I was being a hypocrite. I preached about anger and forgiveness, but I was consumed with worry, and I felt so alone. Not lonely, but alone. God knew I didn't want a broken home, but I didn't want to constantly wonder when this abuse would trigger again. It was making me sick.

In the midst of all this madness, God remained my only reliable source of relief. He was bigger than any problem I was facing, and I knew I was at His mercy, so I gave this to Him. I had no idea what my future looked like, but God did, and I was tired of worrying. I wanted happiness again. I wanted my focus back.

I thought about Amie's death. It wasn't until weeks after she died that I learned that Seth had been physically abusive toward her. Only twice. He'd never punched her, or kicked her, or hit her with an object. He'd never tried to strangle her. She was never hospitalized for domestic abuse. But toward the end of their ten-year relationship, he did tie her down and threaten to kill her. Only once. A few weeks later, when he realized she was breaking up with him for good, he delivered on his threat.

Drew was the only family member who hadn't received any professional help since Amie was murdered, and without a doubt it showed. On the contrary, I advertised how wonderful my counselors had been guiding me through, which included professional therapists besides Fr. Ebuka. I would not be ashamed of saying I had sought help. That was what they were there for, and it sure beat going down the wrong path on my way to recovery.

I put my pencil down to switch gears. I picked up a book and tried taking my mind off of my mind. In the pile of books was *Led by Faith* by Immaculee Irigagiza that I had read a few years back, and without hesitation, God showed me his words through her story.

> Yet, God expected us to be happy, and to find our happiness by filling our hearts with His love. Jesus told us this in JOHN 15:9–11: "As the Father has loved me, so have I loved you. Now remain in my love. If you obey my commands, you will remain in my love, just as I have obeyed my Father's commands and remain in His love. I have told you this so that my joy may be in you and that your joy may be complete."

With those words in that moment, my joy somehow was in fact complete.

CHAPTER 55

Wow! This afternoon, I received the good news that Drew had scheduled an appointment with a trauma-grieving counselor for the next week. He also scheduled for us to meet with a marriage counselor. Thank you again, dear Lord! Regardless of what happens to my marriage, it made no sense for Drew to suffer as he was and remain a danger to himself and society.

I didn't know why I got surprised when God answered my prayers. After all, He is God, and He promised to be faithful to those who loved Him.

CHAPTER 56

Anger plays a necessary roll to evolve from trauma. As long as we remain aware of the discipline it takes to not allow our anger to transform into harmful destruction, it can become a springboard to achieve adequate wisdom toward emotional resilience.

—Nora Greyson's journal

I opened the door to let Olive out and found him sitting on the steps of our back deck. "What are you doing here?" I asked. "Where's your car?"

"Can we talk? I miss you so much. I can't take this. My car's at the town garage getting the brakes repaired. They told me it would be a few hours," Drew said.

"So how did you get here?"

"I walked."

"All the way from the town garage?"

"Yes."

"Drew, that must have taken you—"

He waved a hand. "The walk took nothing. What it gave me was perspective. I dropped the car off at six yesterday, just before closing. I wasn't planning on walking all the way here. I just wanted to go for a walk to clear my head, and before I knew it, just as I was approaching Knights of Sunset's Hotel, it started to get dark. I went inside, grabbed dinner, showered, and rested. I started walking again this morning around five."

"Why?"

"Yesterday afternoon was the party for Mia." He glanced at me.

I suddenly remembered our invitation to Mia's graduation.

"I told Raymond that it would be too awkward for us to go together since we're separated, and I didn't want to go by myself. I didn't want to go without you. Raymond took it offensively. He came home from the party around four drunk and barely able to walk from his car to the house. He fell in his driveway."

"Is he okay?"

"Yes, he's fine, but I couldn't get him up off the ground, and Falene was still at the party helping Mia. I had to call an ambulance for assistance because he was breathing so irregularly. It was embarrassing especially with all the neighbors watching."

I didn't respond, but I knew the feeling. Karma was relentless.

"I don't belong there, Nora. I belong here with you and Toby. I was doing so well. We were happy. You were happy, right?"

I paused for a moment before answering, "Yes."

"I know I said I'd never drink again, and I messed up. I know I did. Amie's death threw me way backward. I wish none of this had ever happened. I can't live without you. I love you and Toby so much. All I do is stare at pictures of us on my phone and wish I were home with you. I'd walk to you from anywhere just to be next to you. I love you. I mean it. I love you, and there's no way I'm going to let our marriage fail. I can't lose you," Drew said passionately and then looked down for a moment as if trailing off in deep thought. "I'm doing the right thing by getting help. You should know that my grieving counselor has been really good. I realize I handled this the wrong way, and I'm sorry. I'll do whatever it takes to fix this. I can't stand living with Raymond and Falene. I want us back together."

Before lunch, I drove Drew back to the garage. Through the rearview mirror, I saw the most hopeful look on Toby's face.

"Daddy's not coming home yet, Toby. He just stopped by to visit." I said matter-of-factly. Toby let his chin lower and glanced at me with big, sad eyes.

Later that night, I received over twenty-seven text messages from Drew telling me he was sorry and wanted to come home.

CHAPTER 57

I knocked on the door.

"Hello," he answered and welcomed us inside. Fr. Ebuka had returned from his trip to Nigeria and had begun ministering at his new location. It was the first time we were seeing him outside church and for me also outside his office. It felt good to be in his presence again.

With my arms full of bags, I entered the kitchen with Toby. And that was strange. For some reason, I hadn't thought a priest would have had a kitchen, but where else would a priest have food prepared? I knew they lived in rectories, but I never thought of a rectory as a home with the usual rooms.

"Where do you sleep?" Toby asked him.

"In a bedroom. Where else would I sleep?"

"That's good," Toby said. "You're a nice person, so I hoped you didn't sleep outside."

Father laughed. "Thank you, Toby. I think you're nice too."

So apparently, I wasn't the only one who thought priests were mysterious, magical, superhuman creatures who didn't need to eat ... or sleep.

We had brought a few housewarming items, and I offered some decorating ideas as we helped tidy up his dining area. And then we sat for lunch. I had prepared steak, Toby's favorite, and as news to us, also Father's favorite.

As we ate, Toby's curiosity continued. "Are you married?"

"No."

"Do you want to be married?"

"No."

"Why not?"

"Because those are the rules."

Toby took a few more bites of his steak; I could see his mind working up new questions.

"What's the worst thing you ever did?"

"Toby! That's not polite," I said feeling a bit embarrassed.

"It's okay. He's just curious. Well, one time, my mother gave me money to buy school books with, but I gambled the money away. But I had such a loving mother. When I told her what I had done, she gave me more money for my books. I was so thankful. I never gambled my book money again."

Toby took another bite of steak and pondered. And then ... "Do you have kids?"

"Yes, hundreds."

The frozen look on Toby's face was priceless.

CHAPTER 58

And we know that in all things God works for the good of those who love Him, who have been called according to His purpose. (Romans 8:28 NIV)

It was an exceptional feeling to tune into a world larger than our own. My problems suddenly seemed to minimize even if for only a moment. By embracing His beautiful distractions in my way, God became more open to doing His work without my distractions in His way.

He is the Alpha and the Omega, the full circle. When I align with Him and through Him, His will becomes my will and my giving becomes my gift, thus completing His purpose. It's an amazing place to be.

Draped from the ceilings were enormous crystal chandeliers that illuminated the lustrous Italian tiled floors that guided me into the hall. Excitement enveloped my being. It was my first night out with adults, and with the promise of exceptional comedians, great company, and a buoyant atmosphere, there was no denying the excitement.

Most of the female volunteers including myself wore beautiful Nigerian dresses that had been handmade by Fr. Ebuka's cousin Adaeze, who had flown in from Nigeria to support the night's event.

We surrounded her and thanked her for making our dresses as they suited the cultural feel for the evening.

The banquet overflowed with hundreds of magnanimous people. Raffled items including fine art lined the main wall along with a large variety of generously assembled gift baskets and gift certificates to several specialty shops among many other highly desirable items. The comedians were hilarious. We laughed so hard that we cried. After the second social hour, a live auction was held that raised several thousand dollars.

Fr. Ebuka spoke.

"While I was an elementary school student, I would walk to school. During those times, I would witness widows and orphans living in the most inhumane and gut-wrenching conditions. With no education or skills that could allow the mothers to earn some income, they had lost all hope for survival. These horrific circumstances led some of them to their deaths while others suffered in surroundings filled with disease and constant hunger.

"Once I became an ordained priest, my mission was to try to protect these women and seek ways to allow them to live with some dignity. Alleviating their burdens was off to a slow start in the beginning. All I was capable of giving them was all that had been given to me outside my own basic needs for food, clothing, and shelter. At that time, this was only a monthly amount of a hundred dollars. Trying to spread that throughout the always growing number of women and children involved was frustrating for me, but as they themselves testified, it did indeed reignite their hope in great measure.

"Sadly, many mothers in this part of the world don't have the privilege of holding their babies before they themselves would die due to lack of medical care during childbirth, and many children would not live past age five also due to lack of medical care.

"Although we currently treat thousands of patients yearly with our team, it's my ultimate goal to foresee a permanent hospital building so these poor, suffering people can receive health care services year around."

I had heard of the horrible conditions that people in Third World countries lived in, but to be directly involved and seeing lives transformed was an entirely different experience. The six parishioners who had accompanied Father on his peregrination spoke about their remarkable time in Nigeria, and the audience became overwhelmed with inspiration by their demonstrations.

Father's eloquent speech to promote a more egalitarian society in Nigeria ended with promising fundraising results that exceeded $35,000. It finished with a recap of how much further we had to go until we were able to assure a structural panacea.

Before the night closed, Father led in heartfelt, thankful prayers for all the members, sponsors, volunteers, and donors. It was a night that will live in my memory forever.

CHAPTER 59

He holds the grace and wisdom to bring home what
is lost, and a stairway to redeem a fresh spirit.
—Nora Greyson's journal

October 2018

In the cool morning air, fallen leaves crunched under our feet as we
walked toward the church. Usually, only the name of the deceased
was mentioned when requested during a Catholic Mass, but Fr.
Ebuka in his goodness had made that day extraordinarily unique
and special.

Drew, Toby, and I attended. It was nice to have our family whole
again for a church service. The pews filled, and opening prayer
began. Father called us into the aisle. He offered a benediction for
the peaceful repose of Amie's soul and healing of our family.

"Thou shall not kill," Father began to preach. The church fell
silent as he continued his message before returning to the altar
and we returned to our seats. I looked at Father from the pew and
wiped away my tear. The choir sang a beautiful version of "Amazing
Grace." Father sat still and held his gaze. And then he lifted his hand
and wiped away his tear.

When the song came to an end, parishioners quietly walked up to us and surrounded us with solace and prayer. It was an incredible moment of consolation and God's reassuring care.

After the homily, Father asked us to the altar. "Bow your heads for special blessings," he said.

When he finished, we sat, and Mass resumed in its traditional order. Before ending, he mentioned for a third time, "This Mass was offered in memory of Amie Greyson."

He had gone above and beyond to alleviate the heavy burden of pain we were carrying, and I was very thankful for his dedication and support and for honoring our family in such a compassionate way.

As soon as we left the parking lot, Drew said, "I really enjoyed today and finally getting to meet Fr. Ebuka."

That was so good to hear.

CHAPTER 60

The aroma of pancakes and bacon rose into our bedroom and woke me. He quietly walked in with a cup of coffee and a soft smile. He placed the cup on our nightstand, knelt beside me, and gently wrapped his arms around me. His warm hug felt so good in the coolness of the early morning fall temperature. The typical New England weather had returned to late summer-like the previous night, before the heat of day left, we had forgotten to turn up our thermostat.

"Good morning, sweetheart," he whispered and kissed my forehead.

Thump, thump, thump. I heard Toby tromping down the hall. He burst into our bedroom with excitement and said, "These are for you, Mommy!" with both hands wrapped around a huge bouquet of long-stem roses. He stretched his arms out as far as they could go as if he couldn't wait to give them to me.

Drew always surprised me with sweet gestures of love. Sometimes, he handed them to Toby to deliver, which of course made them even sweeter.

Two days earlier, Drew had moved back home. After all our family had been through in dealing with Amie's horrific death, the last thing we should have been was apart.

We anticipated our first marriage counseling appointment the next afternoon. He came highly recommended from a reliable source, and I felt optimistic that he would guide our marriage in the right direction.

CHAPTER 61

There's a chemical called leucine-enkephalin found in emotional tears that isn't in any other forms of tears. When we cry, this hormonal chemical releases and reduces our emotional pain, cleansing our bodies from toxins and results in an improved mood. I'm glad to have stumbled upon this finding because crying is all I seem to do, but at least I won't run out of tears. According to American Academy of Ophthalmology, we produce fifteen to thirty gallons of tears yearly.

—Nora Greyson's journal

We sat next to each other on a firm leather sofa. His office was a soothing, warm, sandy color with minimal art work and dim light. He asked some general demographic questions and then a few personal questions.

"What brings you here today?"

"What do you feel your role is as a husband?"

"What do you feel your role is as a wife?"

"What was your relationship like with your parents in your childhood?"

"What is it like now?"

"Do you want your marriage to work?"

"Yes," Drew answered reaching for my hand, and I took his.

Mr. Hemmingway requested individual meetings for the following week. I attended one day with him alone and Drew the next. A week later, Drew and I met with him for the second time together. He spoke with us briefly about surface-level concerns and then looked down for a moment in silence. He looked up and said, "I have to be very honest with you both. I'm very uncomfortable continuing these sessions. I recommend individual counseling for about six months before returning here. My fear is ..." He looked directly at me. "I'm not saying he's going to kill you, but I'm not saying he won't, and I don't want to be responsible for triggering that emotion with the way I prefer to counsel my clients."

We walked out of his office with our heads down.

"I can't believe he said that," Drew said.

I didn't respond.

PART VI

THE FIAT END

Alongside every romantic love song are loose stitches of a poem that sing the opposite tune. It only took one tug of instinct and courage for the bloody string of deceit to unravel.

—Nora Greyson's journal

CHAPTER 62

Narcissistic personality disorder (NPD) is a personality disorder characterized by a long-term pattern of exaggerated feelings of self-importance, an excessive craving for admiration, and struggles with empathy. People with NPD often spend much time daydreaming about achieving power and success, and the perceived injustice of failing to do so. This is a pattern of obsessive thoughts and unstable sense of identity, often to cope with a subpar real life. People with the diagnosis in recent years have spoken out about its stigma in media, and possible links to abusive situations and childhood trauma. Such narcissistic behavior typically begins by early adulthood, and occurs across a broad range of situations.

—Wikipedia

Drew was always the one to intercept the mail. It just so happened that one day when a particular bill was delivered, he wasn't home to retrieve it. There appeared a hotel charge on his credit card statement. Denial filled me. I'd already had all I could take, so I wasn't willing to accept another blow. He couldn't possibly be having an affair especially at a time like this.

"That was the night I left Raymond's house after he returned from Mia's party drunk," Drew explained.

I recalled him telling me that he had left his father's house to get away from it all and had stayed at a hotel for the night, and I was glad for that memory so much so that I wouldn't even connect it to God answering my prayer that I had recited a few weeks prior when I asked Him if Drew was having an affair. The need for confirmation sat in the back of my mind like an elephant, so I did the only rational thing I could think to do. I prayed for clarification.

CHAPTER 63

It is the gracious voice of God Who disturbs me when I'm tempted to settle for the familiarity of sameness even when it lies in its own danger. Blessed are His hands in which I find rescue and rest.

—Nora Greyson's journal

November 2018

Our dining room table was loading up with a beautiful spread of holiday favorites including roasted garlic mashed potatoes, sausage and sourdough stuffing, sautéed parmesan green beans, Nantucket corn pudding, prosciutto-wrapped asparagus, cinnamon-maple-pecan butternut squash, fresh baked cranberry bread, homemade honey butter dinner rolls, a romaine salad with dried cherries, almond slices, feta, avocado, and lemon wedges, homemade apple-cranberry sauce, and the biggest, fattest, perfectly golden twenty-three pound turkey that can ever be imagined.

Drew and Toby stood closely with matching football aprons and helped with preparations while the Macy's Thanksgiving Day parade played in the background. "Look, Daddy! There's the Pokémon float!" Toby said excitingly while pointing at the television.

The glow of the fireplace offered a warm addition to the festive autumn decorations of pumpkins, sunflowers, and pine cones on the mantel and throughout our home.

The doorbell rang. "I'll get it!" Toby said and ran to the door.

"Happy Thanksgiving!" Falene said with a smile holding a bowl of eggnog. She placed it down and leaned over. "You're getting so big!" she said and gave Toby a hug.

Mia entered with a dish of chocolate chip cookies. "Hey, Toby," she said and walked past to greet Drew and me in the kitchen.

Kelsa was visiting for the holidays. She and Leann were on their way with their delicious homemade pies—one pumpkin, one high-top apple, and one heavenly chocolate cream.

Before we began, we bowed our heads and joined hands as Toby led in a Thanksgiving prayer. "O bountiful God, You have blessed us immeasurably with family, friends and an abundance of food. We thank You for these lovely gifts and ask that You will find a way to take care of those who are less fortunate. As we fondly recall past holidays with Aunt Amie, we ask You to continue to grant her rest in Your heavenly peace and reunite us when our time on earth is through, amen."

"Thank you, Toby. That was beautiful," I said.

We sat at the table for hours savoring each course and recalling past times with Amie. Drew was frequently distracted by his cell phone. He quietly walked to and from the table throughout the day until finally announcing that he was tired from his long shifts at work and excused himself to retreat to our bedroom.

Standing in our foyer as the evening came to an end, Kelsa said to me, "I hope Drew's okay. We barely saw him today."

"I hope so too. I'll check on him in few minutes," I replied.

"Let me know how he is and if you need anything."

"I will. Thank you."

I sent them away with generous containers of leftovers, and I smiled thankful for their company.

With Raymond and Falene on one couch resting and Mia and Toby on the other playing video games, I walked into our bedroom to check on Drew. He quickly stuffed his phone in his pocket as I entered. I sat next to him on our bed.

"Hey, is everything okay?" I asked gently.

"Yeah, just tired," he responded as he covered a yawn with one hand.

"Okay, just rest. The girls helped with most of the cleaning already anyway. I'll go and finish up."

"Okay, thanks," he replied lying on his back with hands jammed in his sweatshirt pocket.

I leaned over and kissed his cheek and then went back to the kitchen. The day had been long but enjoyable, and I was grateful that we were back together as a family again.

CHAPTER 64

The first exposure of one's true identity is the only exposure worth counting on.
—Nora Greyson's journal

It was 3:30 in the morning after Thanksgiving. For some reason, I couldn't sleep. I got out of bed and turned on my cell phone. The battery was almost depleted. I reached for the charger plugged into Drew's phone.

Ping. There was a notification. *That's odd. Who in the world could be texting my faithful husband at this hour?* And then I swiped his phone. Several text messages appeared from someone named Heidi: "I need you. It's so cold outside. My so-called husband is horrible. I wish you were here instead of him." "I miss your warm body against mine." "I love you babe, and I'll love you forever."

As I was reading, new messages continued to arrive.

Ping. "I wish you were here loving me."

Ping. "Remember my touch. I think about us being together all the time. I'm so in love with you, Drew."

Ping. "I can't sleep. I can't wait to be in your arms again baby I neeeed you," followed by ten emoji lip prints.

Zombie-like, I took Drew's cell phone and went to the kitchen.

Raymond and Falene were sleeping in the room next door. Again.

I squeezed Drew's phone so hard that I heard a crack. Quiet tears streamed uncontrollably down my face. I heard him snoring from outside our bedroom door, and my fury ran like a schizophrenic centipede that had just been forced from a lazy sewer pipe.

Between 3:30 and 5:30 that morning, fifteen additional text messages came through all confirming an affair. His surreptitious life had been revealed.

Breathe.

I tried to weigh some rational options, but my head was caving in and giving birth to a dangerous organ that was protruding so far out that I could almost grab its slimy fangs and smash it with a hammer. I could have gone charging into our bedroom, slam his phone down his throat, drag him outside in his underwear, lock the door behind me, and burn all his clothes in the fireplace.

Breathe.

One thing I could say for sure about our marriage was that it never lacked passion. Just the opposite was true even after our being together for eighteen years. When Drew suddenly grew distant, I thought it was because of Amie's tragic death. How could I have guessed otherwise? It wasn't every day that your twin sister got murdered.

Breathe.

The clock was ticking. I started mentally preparing myself for the day realizing that if I confronted him right then, it would surely cause a disturbance to say the least, and Toby might forever link the holiday season to the separation of his family life. I didn't want that. I had to find a way to pretend I knew nothing.

CHAPTER 65

It was 7:00 a.m. I started the coffee. Coffee went well with sudden divorce. Drew walked up to me in the kitchen. "Good morning, sweetheart," he said as he wrapped his arms around me.

Breathe. Think of Toby. Don't ruin the holidays for him.

I welcomed Drew with arms wide opened and held onto him before gently pulling back and smiling. "Good morning." I poured him a cup of coffee.

After breakfast, Raymond, Falene, and Mia went home.

In keeping with our day after Thanksgiving family tradition, Drew, Toby, and I drove to a Christmas tree farm to cut down our tree.

Suppress, I remind myself. *You'll have a chance this evening to confront Drew after Toby goes to his sleepover.*

"Daddy! Look at this one!" Toby proudly held his toy chain saw in the air as if ready to claim his prize.

Smiling, Drew looked at me. "What do you think?"

"Looks great," I replied cheerfully.

Drew cut it down, and Toby scampered by his side giggling happily over his find. Through the fields of snow we walked, and my façade hid the pain I bore knowing that I would never see Drew and Toby in this way again, that this would be our last family Christmas tree together.

With our perfect Christmas tree tied to the bed of a borrowed pickup, we headed home.

Out of absolutely nowhere, Toby asked about the Ten Commandments. "Can you remind me of them, Mommy?"

I couldn't resist this opening and skipped the first few to gloat in the invitation of the seventh, but to ease into it, I recited the sixth commandment first.

"Thou shalt not kill."

"Thou shalt not commit adultery."

"What's adultery?" Toby asked.

"I'm glad you asked." And I really was. You can't even begin to imagine. "When God joins a man and women together in marriage, it's considered a holy matrimony or the sacrament of marriage. From that point on, the husband is to forever remain faithful, in other words, not have girlfriends, and the wife is expected to forever remain faithful and not have any boyfriends. If the husband or wife fails, it is a great sin against God and hurts Him deeply. God sees everything, Toby, so you can never lie to Him and get away with it. He always sees everything."

As I explained this to Toby, Drew did a minor swerve in the road.

"Everything okay, dear?" I asked.

"Yeah, just tired."

And my gloat was satisfied, but I hated it all the same.

We set up our tree, and as soon as Toby was off to his sleepover, Drew walked toward our bedroom to be alone. Again.

"Drew, can you come back into the living room?"

He came back, but he wasn't happy about it. "What do you want? I'm tired, and I want to lie down by myself for a little while."

"Who's Heidi?"

And in the headlights was a deer named Drew.

"We're just friends."

"I saw the text messages."

For an intense moment, every clock in the house seemed to stop.

"I'm not happy, and I want a divorce," Drew said as he stood. "Heidi was there for me much more than you were after Amie's death," he said while walking away.

I said nothing.

"After you called the police on me twice in the past, I don't trust you anymore. There's nothing left to this marriage. We're through."

I said nothing.

"I want a simple and fast divorce," he demanded as he walked out the door.

After everything else he had done to me, leaving was his only option because I was surely about to throw him out anyway. I spent the following ten minutes shoving all his clothes into garbage bags. I texted him and ordered him to be back at our house before Toby arrived home the next day to decorate the tree with him as we had done for the past seven years as a family.

Drew arrived just minutes before Toby did, barely enough time to get his garbage bags of clothes out of the house before Toby would see what was happening.

I watched the scene unfold but said nothing.

After about an hour, Drew told Toby he had to stay with Raymond again and help him for a while.

And then he left.

Drew didn't return to visit Toby for almost a full month after that. He missed Christmas, and he missed New Years. Toby was devastated. At times, he cried so hard that I would have traded anything in the world to stop his pain. I wanted to erase it. Swallow it. Burn it.

CHAPTER 66

Some people are brought into our lives for the reason to soften the season, and they leave permeate footprints in our hearts. God gives me Marian, and His timing of course was perfect.
—Nora Greyson's journal

I was due to help my new friend Marian develop advertisements for her business, but emotionally speaking, that wasn't going to happen that day.

"I'm sorry I can't stop by your house," I started, and to my surprise and discomfort, I began sobbing.

"What's wrong?"

"I caught my husband cheating. He left."

"How's Toby handling things?"

"He's understandably very confused and upset," I said through my tears.

"Bring him to my house now."

"Why?" I asked. After all, I barely knew this person.

"Because my sister is a child psychologist and she happens to be visiting from Texas for the holidays."

Moments later, Toby and I stood at Marian's door. She welcomed us with open arms; her embrace felt so comforting. She treated Toby as if he were one of her own, and she counseled me as if we had been friends for years though we had just met at Fr. Ebuka's transfer event less than a year previously. She was the kind women who had gently placed her hand on my shoulder.

For the following three weeks, Marian insisted on cooking dinner for Toby and me every night so I could focus on what needed to be done with my life, yet my mind remained overwhelmed and my focus was absent.

One evening when I stopped by her house for dinner, she handed me a bunch of printouts from her computer. "My sister and I spent the day diligently researching a perfect lawyer for your situation, someone who truly looks out for the best interests of children."

I was stunned by her compassion and dedication.

"Thank you so much. I ..." I took the papers slowly from her hand as my words trailed off. I had no doubt that she was a gift from God brought into my life at that exact time for these exact purposes. As grateful as I was, with such uncertainty about my financial future, I regretfully had to decline her offer. "I think I found someone else who offers free consultations. He has good ratings," I explained to her respectfully. "Thank you so much for all your research, though. I truly appreciate your and your sister's efforts."

The next day, Marian called and insisted on paying for the lawyer's consultation fee, which I absolutely rejected. "No way will I accept a single penny from you," I stated, but my voice was kicked under a deaf rug without a chance of survival.

After a quick back and forth argument, she in her all-loving stubbornness said that if I didn't use the particular lawyer she was recommending, it could permanently damage Toby's and my future. In the end, she went over my head and paid the lawyer's consultation fee.

CHAPTER 67

Through his eyes a tear that belonged to God Himself dropped from the realm that holds heaven and earth. It splashed down and rose up forming an upside-down umbrella that caught the pain like a cocoon, and suddenly the rest of the world does not exist. There is only love, and only me in His love.

—Nora Greyson's journal

"I need to see you. Please, if you're able to, make time to visit me today. It's important. It's not something that can be done over the phone," I said.

"Okay, my dear, I'll rearrange my schedule and be at your house this afternoon."

"Thank you, Father."

At my kitchen table, I started to tell Fr. Ebuka about my husband's betrayal through my tears. I felt that my heart would stop beating.

"How could he do this to Toby?"

"How could he do this to *you*, Nora?"

He reached for my arm and held onto it as if trying to secure me and transmit his strength to me. His head lowered. Profound sadness covered his face.

And then we sat silently.

A sorrow shared is a sorrow halved. *Thank you, God, for this priest.*

CHAPTER 68

Drew was missing.

"He's probably with his new girlfriend," I said.

"No. Heidi's here at our house with us," Raymond said and handed the phone to Heidi.

"Hi. I'm sorry about all this. Drew told me he'd been divorced from you for years," she said.

How did Heidi know where Raymond lived? He and Falene had phoned me just the other day to tell me how wrong Drew was for having an affair and that there was no way they would allow any woman at their house to see him.

"How did you meet him?" I asked.

"Through a friend on social media. I'm sorry, but Drew's status said he was single. Things just happened between us even after I realized he was still married."

"Things don't just happen. People don't walk around and suddenly their pants just happen to fall down. How long have you been seeing my husband?"

"Since Amie died."

"I really don't care about your relationship with my husband right now. We have a child. I need to know where his father is, so you better come up with an answer."

"Drew was supposed to meet me, but he never showed up. I don't know where he is."

"He's probably off drinking with his one and only friend Jeff," I replied carelessly.

Drew had never been big on keeping friends. In fact, he'd barely spoken to Jeff during the past several years as far as I knew. He was always either with me or working. At least I thought that was what he was doing when he left our house in the mornings. He never entertained a social life outside of work hours, not even on the weekends even though from time to time I encouraged that.

"No," Heidi said. "Jeff's here with us. None of us heard from Drew all weekend."

"I'm going to go out and look for him," I heard Jeff say in the background.

Sixteen hours and thirty-seven minutes later, Raymond called to say that Jeff had found Drew's car at an abandoned commuter parking lot. He was contemplating suicide.

"Jeff is with him now. He'll be taking him back to his house to talk to him," Raymond said in a tiresome, arrogant tone that suggested he knew Drew would end up needing help just like his mother did when she was alive. "Well, Falene and I were just about to watch golf on TV. Why don't you give us a call tomorrow?" He brushed it off as if his son had only stumbled and merely scratched his knee instead of having spent the evening thinking about killing himself.

After we hung up, I called Drew. "All this drinking you're doing and sleeping around with this new girlfriend isn't helping you, Drew. You need professional help. You need to go to a hospital tonight and talk to someone. They'll either admit you or advise you on how to get help. You need to find a way to get through this for Toby's sake."

"I know. I've just been so upset. I can't take all this stress," Drew said sobbing. "I'll get help, but not like that. Jeff said he'd find me a therapist and go with me to my first appointment. We'll look into it tomorrow morning."

But Drew never got help.

CHAPTER 69

Along came Brandy and the Jerry Springer show.
                                        —Nora Greyson's journal

Ding.

I heard my phone go off, but I didn't answer. I was still trying to overcome the intensity of the previous day.

Ding.

I took Olive for a walk and left my phone home. When I returned, I took a hot shower and grabbed a good book still not looking at my phone.

There was a knock on my door. I opened it until the chain stopped it. Standing on my front steps was a girl with short, bright-pink hair cut above the top of her stretched earlobes and descended into long bangs that traced the sides of her face and drifted below her chin. Her leather jacket hugged her lanky frame. She was tall and thin and had a small, narrow nose and a pasty, pale face that contrasted with her thick black eye liner and bright-red lips. Her hands were shoved in her pockets as if she were digging for security in a pit too shallow to suffice.

"Can I help you?" I asked.

"I've been livin' wit' your husband for the past few weeks. You need to know what a pig he is."

"Who are you?"

"Brandy May, although most people drink brandy when it's cold outside instead of toward the summer months." Her chin rose enough for me to see her eyes full of anger and sadness.

"I work at a liquor store in the same town that Raymond lives in, an' Drew walked in one night an told me you was such a horrible person, you was divorced, but when you was married, you never fed 'em an made 'em sleep on the couch an wouldn't go near 'em and I thought to myself what a good lookin' guy, how could his wife not want to go near 'em, so I offered 'em a few shots of tequila and had some wit' 'em from a bottle I keep for myself. He made me feel so bad for 'em an started talkin' 'bout all the money he makes and I thought to myself dis guy got it goin' on so we went to the back room and had sex then he slept at my trailer that night and he's been livin' wit' me ever since and man I thought he was the one an I introduced 'em to my kids and everythin' but he ain't nuthin' but a liar and a pig an' you need to know the truth 'bout 'em."

Brandy continued to rattle at full speed with understandable hostility. I couldn't get a single word in. Then as if all this weren't hard enough to take in, she confessed that the weekend Drew was missing, he had been with her at Raymond's beach house having sex and drinking all weekend long, and Drew had not been suicidal at all.

She paused and lit a cigarette before continuing in a low, bitter monotone. "Man, I was so curious 'bout you I'd go on social media to look you up and I noticed all these recent picture of you guys together and I thought to myself dis doesn't seem right 'cause Drew told me he's been divorced for years, but there was like no way and then I found several more social media accounts wit' Drew and other chicks and I was like what in the world is going on that's when I knew sometin' was up so I took screen shots and I just sent 'em to your phone before I came here so you would have a heads-up. Man dis is so unbelievable I was like I ain't putting up wit' dis so I noticed the bar he was at in one of his pictures and I went there one night and dis old ugly chick was all over 'em and I thought what an ugly looking hag she was. Man you shoulda seen this chick. She's *ooooold* and flabby it was nasty I was like how could he go wit' her? And it wasn't even the same chick I saw in those pictures on social media and dis was before I realized he was still married to you can you imagine if you saw what I saw?"

Without waiting for my response, Brandy continued with her prattling.

"Anyway I got in Drews face and yelled 'Surprise!' Man you shoulda seen the look on his face his jaw dropped to the ground and that chick started attackin' 'em cryin' and everythin' right there inside the bar. Man, you ain't gonna believe dis but she's married to the owner of that bar that old wrinkled up flabby hag wait til he finds out cuz I'm gonna tell em next he wasn't there that night, but I'll find em and tell em. Man I can't believe how old and ugly dis chick was usually when men cheat it's wit' a younger chick like I'm eight years younger than Drew but what does he see in that nasty old hen she's gotta be like ten years older then 'em. Man, I'm so hurt and I was only wit' 'em for a few weeks I can't imagine how you feel after bein' wit' 'em for all these years."

Brandy filled me in on the numerous times she'd gotten drunk and had sex with my husband cursing him to no end. She said she'd be more than happy to help nail him in court when we divorced. When I finally had an opportunity to speak, I asked her how she had gotten my house address.

"I found it on his GPS. I kicked 'em out of my trailer."

I picked up my phone and looked at the screen shot messages from Brandy. One read, "My sister was just murdered and I'm going through a divorce. I'm so lonely. I wish I could be with you." That had gone to five women. I was so disgusted that Drew had used the tragic way Amie had died to get as many women in bed with him as he could. Brandy couldn't apologize enough to me, and I appreciated her empathy and felt sorry for her as well that Drew had broken her heart too as strange as that might sound. Of all the women involved, she was the only one who had been brave and honest enough to come forward, and I respected her for that.

I unlocked the door chain, stepped outside, and sat on my front steps. "Please have a seat, Brandy. It must have taken you a lot of guts to come here, and I appreciate that."

Surprisingly, she didn't say anything for a while, but she sat. When we finally started talking, it was as if we were talking about someone else's life, and about halfway through, we found a way to turn it into a comic strip of strange events, and we were laughing even though it was no joke. Forty-five minutes into our talk, she asked, "Guess who's callin'," as she looked at her phone. "Hey Drew, guess what? I'm sitting on your front steps hangin' wit' your wife and I'm tellin' her everyting, *ha ha!*"

And then she hung up. And then Drew started calling me. One call, two calls, five calls, fifteen calls. At first I ignored them, but as his calls exceeded forty-five times, I thanked Brandy for coming forward and then I told her she needed to leave.

"Man, you're such a sweetheart. Drew really made you sound like such a nasty person, but there's like no way. Stay safe, an' I'm so sorry this happened to you. Drew don't deserve you!"

The second she left, I checked my messages. Drew was in a drunken rage screaming and threatening that I better not be with Brandy, claiming that she was a dangerous person.

"No way," I responded coolly. "She seemed to really like me. You must have done something to make her mad if you think she could be dangerous."

And then Drew flipped out to the point that I couldn't understand a single thing he was saying. My mind had all it was capable of handling for one night, so I went to Toby's bedroom and got him out of bed, and we left.

CHAPTER 70

Everyone must choose one of two pains: the pain of discipline or the pain of regret.

—Jim Rohn

The test of forgiveness was in front of me again, and the temptation to get even was fierce. A full week had passed since the evening with Brandy.

It was four in the afternoon. That was when Drew and I planned to get together with Toby and talk to him about the divorce.

"I can't make it," Drew called to tell me at 3:45 without any explanation.

"I'm not waiting for you. Toby deserves to know what's going on. I'm telling him as much as I can without letting him know about the affairs. He doesn't need to feel he's been traded in for your cheap women." I hung up and prayed, *God, please grant me the wisdom I need to do this the right way.*

I brought Toby into my bedroom, where there were no Christmas decorations in the background. I didn't want Christmas time to be a reminder of the painful change he was about to endure regarding his family structure.

We sat down at the edge of my bed. I lowered my head to his eye level and softly spoke matter-of-factly. "Toby, Daddy has made some very bad decisions and has done some very dishonest and hurtful things, things that a husband should never do to his wife."

"Are you getting a divorce?" Toby asked.

"Yes," I answered without an extended explanation wanting to keep things straightforward and as simply stated as possible.

Toby threw himself facedown on my bed and sobbed heavily. I cried too. We cried without speaking for a long time. Finally, Toby said, "I knew this was going to happen, but I don't want it to. I want a new daddy, one that won't leave."

"That wouldn't be emotionally healthy for either one of us if I ran out and got you a new daddy right away. It's important right now that we allow some time to heal ourselves without a new person involved in our lives, and it's important to have self-respect. We are both so hurt that we have to be extra careful about how we react to it because we don't want to make a decision that will temporarily make us feel better but make our lives worse in the long run.

I let some silent time go by and rubbed his back. "The most important thing I want you to know is how much I love you and that I will never, ever, *ever* leave you. Not for any reason. And I'm so sorry that this is hurting you so badly."

Toby sat up slowly and hugged me tightly, but I knew in his young confused mind, he was probably questioning if I would never leave him. Especially as I recalled all the times Drew told Toby about Raymond leaving him when he was a child and that he would never do that to his son. I remember saying to Drew at those times, "Be careful whom you hate because you'll end up just like them." Drew would reply behind quiet anger, "There's no way I'd do that to Toby."

The sad truth is that when we really hate others, we spend a lot of time thinking about them and how they have wronged us, and if we aren't careful, we will indeed become like them. The difference between repeating the cycle and breaking it is the difference between allowing our anger and fear to make us better people or remaining in the debilitating aftermath of a bitter, self-focused grudge.

How in the world could Toby trust *me* now? All I could do was allow time to pass to prove to him that I was sincere to my core. I madly wished that an abundance of time would somehow magically speed past him in a moment so he could see for himself that I wasn't going anywhere.

"Does this have anything to do with the night Daddy was yelling and swearing at you outside?"

"That's part of the reason," I said not wanting to elaborate.

"Are you sure you weren't driving the car that killed Auntie Amie?"

"Yes, I'm sure."

"I still think Daddy thinks you were driving the car."

"I can assure you that he doesn't."

I knew then that I needed to tell him the truth about his aunt's death, but not that night. That night had caused him enough pain.

After our talk, we walked into the living room. Our annoying Christmas tree fell over again for the third time that week. I was using bungee cords to keep it upright.

Just before Toby turned on the television, he walked up to me and said, "Let me know if you need anything, Mom."

He seemed so mature and strong. I was so proud of him, and I admired his strength and compassion dearly. But I was the adult. I was supposed to hold him up, not him me.

CHAPTER 71

For this is like the waters of Noah to Me; for as
I have sworn that the waters of Noah would no
longer cover the earth, so have I sworn that I would
not be angry with you, nor rebuke you. For the
mountains shall depart and the hills be removed,
but My kindness shall not depart from you, nor
shall My covenant of peace be removed. (Isaiah
54:9–10 NKJV)

The inspirational sign on her door read, "It's okay to be scared. Being
scared means you're about to do something really, really brave."
—Mandy Hale

"Hi, I'm Attorney Yvette," she said and stood and extended her
hand to me. With only a one-hour time allowance, I briefed her on
my sister-in-law's death, Drew's abuse and affairs, and his neglect
of Toby.

She looked concerned. "How are you emotionally handling all
this?"

"I've received exceptional guidance and support from a priest.
I've also spent some time with a therapist, and I've been mentored
by a few good friends."

I could tell she was a compassionate person, but she also had a professional responsibility and was obligated to lay out the facts.

"I'm sorry to have to say this to you, but since you've made more money than your husband for the majority of the time you were married to him, you'll probably end up having to pay him alimony. In addition, you'll be lucky if you get a small amount of weekly child support. The best I can tell you right now is that if you take the parenting classes and he doesn't, he can never change the amount of child support he has to pay. You should also know that he could take half of your home's worth or at least half of the equity. Your best bet is to see if he'll sign a quitclaim deed and turn the house over to you, but that usually never happens, and I've been doing this long enough to know that people like Drew are certainly the least likely of them all.

"Here are some forms. You'll need to list all your assets including bank accounts. Drew will probably request half of everything. Again, I'm sorry. I wish I had better news for you."

The dark pit of mortifying sludge I already dwelled in seemed to engulf me even more. My eyes began to burn. My throat tightened. I fought back tears. But I had researched her credentials before our meeting and knew she was good and must have been stating the truth.

After her preliminary assessment, her focus shifted to Toby. We agreed that due to Drew's current unpredictable and toxic lifestyle, visitations should be supervised. At the end of our meet, she requested her consultation fee. I handed her the check, which Marian had made out to her. She studied it for a moment. "Who wrote this check?"

"My friend Marian took it upon herself to research a good lawyer for Toby and me. She insisted on you. And then she insisted on paying for today's hour with you."

"I think I know this woman. In fact, she was good friends with my aunt when they lived next to each other several years ago. What church do you attend?"

"Saint Jerome Emiliani."

"I'm on the board at that church. What priest did you see?"

"Fr. Ebuka."

"I know him!" she said with pleasure.

She told me I was in very good hands and had nothing to worry about.

I walked out of her office in a state of frustration and distress for all that was being lost and the uncertainty of my financial future or even if I would have a home to raise Toby in, but I also felt a separate kind of comfort I couldn't explain especially considering the reality of the hard core facts. All I could say was that this couldn't possibly have been a coincidence. There I was a few towns away from mine having met a lawyer who knew my church, my priest, and my friends with no prior evidence for making those connections. God was truly in control and had placed another specific person in my life for a specific purpose, and my emotions restfully resigned in His loving grace. *Trust God*, I reminded myself.

On the way home, I called Marian about the meeting eager to find out if she knew about any of these connections. She answered no, not even the connection between her and Attorney Yvette's aunt. Since Attorney Yvette used her married name, Marian hadn't recognized it. She was delighted by this story, but in her faith and wisdom, she was not the least bit surprised.

CHAPTER 72

But the meek shall inherit the earth, and shall delight themselves in the abundance of peace. (Psalm 37:11 NKJV)

Ding.

It was Adaeze checking in. I was glad to hear from her. She had been sending me daily reminders to be strong in an attempt to deter even the smallest trace of revengeful anger. That day was no different: "My dear friend, I hope this finds you okay. Please focus on controlling your emotions. Keep Toby out of it for now. Let's talk when you are less busy."

She included a video attachment that broke down what spiteful anger did to a person and how it destroyed everything around us. It was ten minutes long, but I watched it all the way through, and I realized I needed the advice.

My emotions were as wild as a coyote under a full moon. When I'd first found out about the affairs, I was half in shock and half-relieved to have a way for Drew to exit my life through his own wrongdoing and guilt. But that night, I was crying uncontrollably. I questioned Drew on how he could have done this to Toby and me. I couldn't catch my breath. The pain of the betrayal felt more than

I could handle. After my initial outburst, I just sobbed unable to speak.

All of the sudden, Drew stopped being defensive and became penitent admitting that everything was a hundred percent his fault. He calmed down and put on an almost soothing voice when he spoke. "Nora, I always felt you could do so much better than me. You can go and marry any man you want, and I really mean anyone. It's just not going to be me because I don't know how to be strong."

Drew's words stung hard. I felt so sad but also that that was the first honest thing he had said to me since this all had begun. I put my hand over my mouth so he wouldn't hear me cry as silence widened thickly in the strange distance between us.

"I don't want anything from you, Nora. I don't even want the house. You can have everything."

Your best bet is to see if he will sign a quitclaim deed and turn the house over to you … Attorney Yvette's words rang in my head. I thought I needed to speak, and I needed to do it right then while Drew was feeling guilty. "Will you meet me in the morning at the town hall to sign the house over to me?"

"Yes," Drew replied without hesitation. He sounded relieved to do this as if it were a way to pay off some of his guilt.

The following morning, he was waiting in the parking lot at the town hall. We signed the quitclaim deed, and I thanked God for His perfect timing, but my heart was aching terribly. *What good is a house if it holds only a broken family?* I wondered.

In the next few weeks, Drew and I sorted out the ownership of our vehicles and bank accounts. When I returned home, I removed him from all credit card accounts and as beneficiary of our insurance policies. The reality between the previous day and that day further confirmed the definite separate futures Drew and I would have, and I was overwhelmed by a range of emotions—from anger to mourning—and then I remembered I was missing only a monster.

Ding. It was Adaeze again in her all-loving persistence. As I slowed my thoughts, I realized if she hadn't been so determined and if I had given into my need to express my anger toward Drew, he and his pride would have never signed the house over to me. Call it what you will, but in my eyes, Adaeze had advised me exactly the way God had intended. If not for that intervention, Toby and I would have lost everything.

CHAPTER 73

Loneliness doesn't claim us through the loss of assurance from people that we once trusted, but instead when we lose sight of our abilities to give. It is within the deceiving trap of self seeking gratifications that loneliness can transform into selfish and malevolence desires.

—Nora Greyson's journal

When a priest is ordained, he chooses a passage from the Bible to live by. "Freely you have received, freely give" (Matthew 10:8 NKJV). These words spread across Fr. Ebuka's cake as we gathered to celebrate his seventeenth year of priestly ordination and his birthday.

"Please don't post this event in the church bulletin," I asked only half-joking as his guest list exceeded two hundred. Thankfully, an abundance of parishioners had extended helping hands.

Some of us knew each other while others were meeting for the first time. The night was magical in a sense, as if we were all rejoining happily at a long overdue family reunion.

Toby proudly guarded the door with an important job of handing out name tags as tables began to overflow. Food was plentifully displayed buffet style, and with our treasured DJs at work, the crowd elated in Father's company. An honorable guest priest paid tribute to the toast, and many others followed by taking turns with the microphone to share their stories and experiences with Fr. Ebuka. Even the youngest children were in awe with veneration.

The evening continued to glow with favorable moments, and all bore witness that one of Father's greatest assets was a rare and special gift—his ability to make all who entered his life feel that they were the only ones who mattered even though we all knew he had no favorites. It was simply his nature to love and live by God's Word to the point that he became Christlike. If we stopped to think about it, wasn't that what all Christians are called to do?

After the evening ended and I was home, I sat in reflection with gratitude for the emotional break from the ruins in my life.

Ding. It was a thank-you text from Fr. Ebuka. He was overjoyed to tell me that he accredited over $15,300 in cash gifts to benefit the continuation of the building of his hospital. I beamed as I was acknowledging this good news especially since this had not been a fundraising event. He had been right from the beginning. Belonging to a charitable organization did indeed provide a tremendous range of undeniable benefits, and becoming involved with his ministry had been the bright light that shined through my darkest and most devastating days.

CHAPTER 74

Forgiveness isn't giving permission to the crime. It doesn't mean forgetting the crime happened, or that we should continue to allow the villain in our lives as I once thought in the beginning of my story. And it isn't based on whether the villain deserves to be forgiven or not.

Forgiveness is based on deciding that we deserve peace.

The criterion of forgiveness says that we will not allow the crime to ruin our life or anyone else's. This is something I have to keep learning. The raw truth is that it doesn't matter who hurts us or how. Ultimately, we are responsible for ourselves.

—Nora Greyson's journal

Drew didn't show up to visit Toby last Saturday. He pushed the visit to Sunday, but didn't show up. He pushed it to Monday, but didn't show up.

Toby was hysterical. "Daddy said he can't come today! Why doesn't he see me or call anymore?"

"I'm so sorry, Toby. I'm ten minutes away. Hang in there. I'll be home before you know it."

My only reasoning that seemed acceptable and at least somewhat honest was to remind Toby that his father up until recently had been working second shift and that even if he had been still living at home, he wouldn't have been able to see Toby or talk to him much anyway.

When I arrived, I found Leann sitting next to Toby rubbing his back as he lay face down on the sofa sobbing. I sat next to him, took him in my arms, and let him cry. Leann and I surrounded him and soothed him for over an hour.

"I want to be an inventor and build a time machine so things can go back to the way they used to be," Toby proclaimed through heavy tears.

"I know you do, Toby. I know, and I'm so sorry that your heart's so broken," I said.

"Nora, I don't know how you do it. This is terrible seeing Toby this way," Leanne said.

"I do it because I love him. I do it because I won't allow him to suffer alone. I do it because he is in fact a very important person and I refuse to allow his father's behavior shape his thoughts any other way."

"Well, you certainly have a very smart young boy. When Drew told him he couldn't visit today because he didn't have money for gas for his car, Toby told Drew how disappointed he was and told him to go get a job."

CHAPTER 75

It is art that makes life, makes interest, makes importance and I know of no substitute for the force and beauty of its process.

—Henry James

I decided never to date again. I didn't even want to entertain that thought, but I did feel it would be nice to be noticed. After all, it had been almost half a year ... or more depending on how you looked at it.

Everyone including my own kid suggested that I go and find a new man, but I had absolutely no desire. All I really wanted was to be left alone. I was worn out, and the pressure of everyone's good intentions was making me feel even more overwhelmed. But sometimes, I was a little curious about what it might be like, so I prayed for God to give me a glimpse just in case some day I felt ready to try to love again.

My first request was that this person would love God above all things especially knowing what I knew about reverence and how weak a person could become without Him. I prayed that he would know what it was like to be betrayed in a marriage and to have suffered a loss similar to mine, and that we would have some interests

ONLY GOD CAN TURN THIS MESS INTO HIS MESSAGES

in common. The prayer was short but precise, and I'm ashamed to admit I didn't expect the assurance I received.

A few days later, I had a hair appointment. When I arrived, the place was empty and mostly dark. The hairdresser took me to his styling cubicle and told me that the salon was usually closed on Mondays but that the owner had asked him to come in for my appointment. As he was looking sadly through my not-so maintained hair, I explained that it was the first time I'd been in a salon in about a year.

"What? Why?"

"Long story."

"There's no one else here if you'd like to talk," he said waving at the empty cubicles.

"That's okay, but thank you."

I stayed quiet for a while before I asked how long he'd been a hairdresser.

"I've been licensed for a few years, but I've been at this for much longer. My ex-wife owned a salon, and I worked with her for a long time." He said they had divorced after she had two affairs, which had been heartbreaking for him. "But I forgave her because that's what a Christian is supposed to do."

"I'm sorry to hear that," I said. I sat in silence and drifted off to the rhythm of the background music. A Michael Bublé song played. "I love his music," I said with a smile.

"Me too."

I mentioned a few other favorite jazz musicians from the UK whom most people in the US weren't familiar with, and to my surprise, he knew them all.

"Before my cousin died, we used to be in plays together. One of the most memorable was about Catholics and Protestants fighting each other, and there was a girl who sat in between them who played her instrument until both sides became peaceful with each other. My cousin played the girl with the instrument, and I was the boy of peace. We were very close."

His story reminded me of how much I used to love going to plays when Drew and I started dating, and I wondered how his cousin had died, but I didn't dare ask. "I'm so sorry for your loss," I said.

A few moments later, I asked if he was Catholic.

"Yes. Before I met my ex, I was in the seminary."

Right in the middle of his doing my hair, I yelled, "You're blowing my mind!" I jumped out of my chair and almost ran out the door chemicals in my hair and all.

"Wait! I'm sorry if I said something to upset you," he said sounding confused, but there was no way I was going to even attempt to explain myself. "Are you sure you don't want to talk? I'm a good listener, and we have at least another half-hour for your hair to set."

"No, but thank you. My story might make you cry. Or I might cry. I'm sorry I was jumpy. You must think I'm nuts."

"No. Don't worry about it. I'm a crier too. People have told me that I wear my heart on my sleeve. I've been divorced for a few years now, but it still hurts."

"Do you mind if I ask you how long you were married?" I asked.

"Sixteen years."

That was how long Drew and I had been married.

Latin music started to play. "This reminds me of dancing," I said thinking of Toby's suggestion that I start dance classes again.

"I love to dance especially in clubs," he said.

Oh how I've wanted to go out dancing! I thought.

After a few more Latin songs, Christmas music played, which was kind of strange in April, but I loved Christmas music, so it didn't bother me.

I noticed him looking out the window. "Sometimes, I love to get lost in music, and I really love Christmas music," he said.

I said nothing but recalled many nights of listening to Christmas music and getting lost in the magic of it while producing works of art. *There's something profoundly healing about letting go and focusing all my energy on art*, I thought.

"Are you married?" he asked as he washed out my hair.

"Sort of," I replied.

"Is that part of your story?"

"Yes, just a part."

"His loss."

"Thank you," I replied, and I meant it.

When I was about to leave, he asked me to wait. "I have something I'd like to show you." He went to retrieve his cell phone. When he returned, he showed me on it the most beautiful pictures of watercolor painted seascapes I have ever seen—absolutely stunning. Then he showed me some sketches he had made of his son, again exceptionally amazing work.

"I love art," he said.

At that point, all I could say was, "Of course you do." I smiled. "Thank you. It was a pleasure meeting you." I looked into his eyes, shook his hand, and left.

While walking to my car, I paused in the parking lot and glanced over my shoulder. Through the large store front window, I saw the nice-looking gentleman I had just had a remarkable encounter with smile at me as he sat on a stool. When he offered a gentle nod, I wondered if he knew he was yet another angel God had placed in my life in His perfect timing.

The Lord is merciful and gracious, slow to anger and abounding in compassion and loving kindness. (Psalm 103:8 AMP)

All I had asked for was a glimpse. To meet someone who loved God, had some things in common with me, and had an understanding about my series of unfortunate events. And I'd gotten exactly what I'd prayed for. Although my soul rejoiced in satisfied hope, a part of me was shadowed with guilt.

Trust God. I recalled thinking that I did. But then I realized that I had tested Him, and that part I was ashamed of.

CHAPTER 76

You don't have to see in order to believe. You have to believe in order to see. Believe that God is the highest Love. He is your Guide, your Protector, your Healer, and He created you to be the salt of the earth. Believe this as if your life depends on it, for indeed it does.

—Nora Greyson's journal

"There have been some problems during lunch period with another classmate who was caught calling names and shooting a rubber band at Toby. We want you to know that we're addressing this matter with this child's parents, but Toby has had a hard time settling back down in class, and I had to move his desk. He became very upset and hit his head with his fists several times, and then he banged his head on his desk very hard, which alarmed me enough to notify the school nurse. She rushed to our classroom, but Toby refused to allow her to check him out. He kept calling himself names and hitting himself. We had to get the school psychiatrist to calm him down. In addition, twice this past week, Toby assumed he was being left out of fun activities by his peers and became aggressive until he was in a position he felt he could control," his teacher said.

On my way to pick up Toby from school, I recalled all the recent times he'd sought negative attention at home. I wondered how I had missed that. He was certainly going through some very difficult moments trying to deal with extreme, sudden disappointments and the pain of his father's and his classmates' rejection. He had a therapist, but that didn't seem to be helping although no fault of hers. It wasn't until recently that I realized I should have had Toby with a male therapist, not a female. One who looked at least somewhat similar to his dad.

Breathe.

I loved him and knew I had to redirect him even though I wished I could just put him in a bubble full of cotton far away from this world where no one could ever hurt him again. But that wasn't happening. The only realistic way to proceed as a parent was to not allow Toby to think he could misbehave based on the negative actions of others.

"Toby, what your dad did to you does not change who you are as a person. You're still wonderfully you. Don't ever think your dad's destroyed your life. Don't ever give him or anyone else that much power over you. He left himself long before he ever left us. He ruined his own life, not ours. You are *not* like your father in this way, and you will never be, not ever.

"Your life isn't ruined. My life isn't ruined. Our lives have just changed, and change is the only thing we can ever rely on completely outside of God. But it's not always a bad thing, so don't be afraid of it. Change as you will see can be very beautiful, Toby."

"I hate change, Mommy. I want things back how they used to be."

He stared out his bedroom window. The same window that once reflected a kind and loving father who had blown kisses to him in the early mornings.

"Most people hate change because they think they're afraid of it, but what they're really afraid of is not knowing what the change will bring. If they knew the change would give them a better future, they'd be happy about it. I know that right now, it feels like your life and the pain you feel is stuck in this heartbreaking time, but change will happen again and probably for the better. All that happened was out of your control. Maybe that's why you're reacting so quickly and forcefully the second you see things not going your way. It's understandable that you're trying to protect your feelings from more disappointment and that you probably want to feel a sense of control again somehow, but you must always think about how your actions will affect the outcome of your choice. I know you, Toby. You have a good heart, and you don't want to hurt yourself or anyone else. Your dad cannot take that from you unless you let him."

"I don't want that, Mommy."

"Then next time, be sure to think before you act. Life here on earth is just a day in school. Some lessons we will like and some we won't, but either way, the day is short. You'll see. Through it all, you must believe that God loves you because He is Love, and He doesn't make mistakes. What I'm saying is that when He made you, He did it on purpose and did it in His own image. As a reflection of God, you're here to love, not to hate."

That could be difficult for any struggling adult to grasp let alone an abandoned child. These words were so similar to those I tried to share with Drew, but unfortunately, he wasn't receptive. My hope was in the malleability of the youthful mind.

I thanked God for His wisdom, and I thanked Him that He didn't change.

I walked down to my basement to retrieve the laundry, and there was a flood. It was Friday evening right before Easter weekend. I shut off the water and called a plumber. Apparently, a pipe in the kitchen had broken. A disaster cleanup company arrived with dry vacs and dehumidifiers, but the damage to my kitchen was already done.

That was all I can say about that day.

CHAPTER 77

Self-control is strength. Calmness is mastery. You have to get to a point where your mood doesn't shift based on the insignificant actions of someone else. Don't allow others to control the direction of your life. Don't allow your emotions to overpower your intelligence.

—James Allen

June 2019

It was Father's Day weekend. Drew said that he didn't have gas money to drive to my house and that his new job had lasted only for a day.

"Mommy, today is Daddy's special day. Will I be able to see him?" Toby asked.

"Yes. I'll take you to see your dad at Raymond and Falene's."

The visit went well. Drew and Toby played a few games and spent some quality time together, but it felt like someone else was there especially because a strange car was parked in their driveway and the back bedroom door was locked even though that was where they kept a basket of toys for Toby to play with when he visited.

Toby was not allowed into that room during our visit.

Raymond stood in his tight golf clothes on his exaggerated wobbly cane and in an almost too cheerful way talked about some upcoming sporting events that he and Falene were planning to attend. I nodded politely but said nothing, and I was relieved that after a while, we found room for other small talk. I had no desire to reestablish a relationship with them, but I didn't want the visit to be tense for Toby's sake.

The next day, I woke to a voice message. It was Falene saying that she had loved seeing Toby and me and hoped we could get together again soon. I didn't respond.

The following day, I received a text message from Drew saying he hated his life without me and missed the old days. I didn't respond.

Later that day, I was deleting old photos of Drew from my social media account and noticed how his looks had changed tremendously. He had gone from being very well kept, clean cut, and in great physical shape to a thick, unruly bearded, bloated person dressed in rags. The change started gradually after that night of his first arrest back in 2016. It was as if he'd grown a layer of a completely different human being over his old self physically and psychologically. That was when his personality had started shifting from a husband eager to please and never wanting to be apart from me to someone who would push me out of the way and mumble insults under his breath. I wondered if he had had his first affair back then.

Drew in his cryptic way had multiple social media accounts, one with him, Toby, and me and others with him posing with and coveting additional women.

I never posted a single thing about my family's deterioration on social media. I never understood the value of doing that.

A therapist once told me that Drew might have felt he had to eliminate everyone and everything that connected him to his life when Amie was alive and replace it with anyone and anything else he could. Whether that was true or not, at least it was something that makes some sense even though it was no excuse.

CHAPTER 78

With temperatures soaring above 95 and thick haze filling the air, it was no wonder that Toby was excited about jumping into the large swimming pool secluded by tropical palm trees though we lived in Rhode Island. Pizza trucks and flaming oversized grills were at the front of their beach house, where an enormous veranda sat overfilled with a bounce house and children's games.

Falene was glad we had accepted the Fourth of July party invitation and welcomed us with open arms. I was going to reject the invite, but I felt that Toby could benefit from spending some time with his cousins.

As I approached her, I noticed a light bruise on her cheek but said nothing. She assured me that Drew was not welcomed though I'd never expected that.

Out of the corner of my eye, I saw Raymond stealing a glance. He approached cautiously. "May I talk to you?" he asked.

"Sure," I answered with a feeling of regret right after the word left my mouth. I wanted to disappear among other family members, but there was no escaping Raymond and Falene.

"I kicked Drew out. All he does is drink—morning, noon, and night—sometimes starting as soon as he wakes up. Last week, he punched some big holes in my walls. Don't ever take him back no matter what. I know him much better than you do, and he's weak minded just like his mother was. You have all of us on your side, and you have a lot going for you. You can do so much better than Drew." My thoughts instantly reflected back to Drew's words just before he agreed to give me the house. *"Nora, I always felt you could do so much better than me. You can go and marry any man you want, and I really mean anyone. It's just not going to be me because I don't know how to be strong."* I wondered how many times Raymond spoke to Drew this way before Drew believed it.

Raymond put a hand on my shoulder and looked at me sternly. Sweat traced his forehead, and his body shook with intensity as he held himself up with his cane. "I don't ever want to hear that you've taken him back, and I mean it, not ever. You're an excellent mother to Toby. All that Toby has become is due to your guidance. Drew will mess up his life and send you two into a living nightmare. Keep him away and move on. I'd rather see Drew drink himself to death in the streets than to ever see you get back together with him."

My head snapped upright in disbelief of what I had just heard Raymond say about his only son especially after losing his only daughter. As much as it would seem that I should have been happy about Drew's family turning against him, I knew that wasn't right. Although Raymond clearly disapproved of how Drew was living, he had had a major part in influencing his behavior, but I didn't hear him taking any responsibility for that.

"I don't know how you do that," I said. "You've always been so selfishly absent and unpredictably careless about Drew to the point that he doesn't even call you Dad. You've shaped him to be just like you, not like his mother but you, and then you criticize him for it. He spent his entire life trying to fit into yours only to be rejected time and time again. It's a miracle that any emotions outside of anger could fit into his soul. I promise you that I have more self-respect than to ever consider taking Drew back, but there's no way I'll force Drew out of Toby's life as long as he visits him when he's sober."

Raymond looked at me with intense eyes, "Whatever. It's not my fault he's like this. My father was in and out of my life when I was growing up, and I turned out just fine."

CHAPTER 79

Cursed is the one who perverts the justice due the stranger, the fatherless, and widow. (Deuteronomy 27:19 NKJV)

August 2019

Drew came to visit, but since he had lost another job, he showed up drunk. I didn't dare call him out on it. The visit was short, less than an hour, and he barely spent any time with Toby. When he decided he was ready to leave, Toby clung onto the back of his car.

"Toby, get down," Drew demanded.

Toby started moaning. "Daddy, don't go! I don't get to see you enough anymore. I haven't seen you since Father's Day. Please, Daddy, *nooooo*."

Toby clenched harder turning the tips of his fingers white with pressure. He buried his face in the top of Drew's car. "I can't let you go, *Daaadyyyyy!* Don't go! Don't *leeeeaaave!*" Toby started crying as he repeated this agonizing plea. With every ounce of his strength, he held onto his dad's car in hopes of saving the sacred livelihood of their relationship.

It must have been a miracle that Toby's cries shocked Drew into what seemed to be a moment of soberness. Suddenly, Drew was able to offer some small talk of compassion even if it was just for the sake of bribing. "Toby, I'll always be here for you. I'll start visiting two to three times a week if you want. Come on down. I love you, and I don't want you upset."

But Toby wasn't buying it.

After a little more time and effort, we were able to detach Toby from Drew's car, and then Drew drove away.

In attempt to run after his dad, Toby tripped and landed hard in our driveway. He looked up only to see taillights distancing farther and farther away, and his mouth opened as wide as it could into a heart-shattering scream, *"Daaaadyyyyyyyy! Waaaaaaaiiiiiit!"*

Rushing to his rescue, I knelt and lifted him off the asphalt. "Let's go inside," I gently suggested.

"Nooooo! I want Daaaaaaaaaady!"

His torso stiffened like a wooden board, and his fingers dug at the ground he was laying on as if trying to find something, anything left behind to pull his father back, or a reminder to carry with him, something to keep.

But there was nothing.

I somehow picked him up and carried him into our living room. I gently placed him on the couch, where he threw himself facedown and remained in that position sobbing for the next four hours. Yes, four hours. It was the most heart-wrenching moment of my life. My mind, my spirit, and everything in me shattered. What was left of me? How could I possibly help my son? I felt that I could die and not know the difference. *God, I don't know how to live this life.*

I leaned over him and held him. I was crying too. I couldn't help it. *Be strong*, I told myself.

"This is my fault! I'm so ashamed!" Toby yelled in between sobs. "I'm responsible for not stopping Daddy from acting the way he did the night you had to call the police. If I could relive that day, I'd have stopped him from yelling and swearing at you. When I build my time machine, I'm going to change everything!"

"No, Toby, you wouldn't have stopped anything because you couldn't have," I softly said.

"*Yes I could have!*"

"No, you couldn't, and it wasn't your job to protect me. It's my job to protect you. And it isn't your job to make sure your father acts the right way. That's his job. Your only job is to be a kid."

Toby continued to sob. I lifted his face in my hands and rested my forehead on his. "Toby, I want to share something very important with you, some advice from your very wise great-grandmother. Once when I was a little girl, a bit younger than you are, I was going through a difficult time too, and she held my face in her gentle hands just as I'm holding yours now, and she said, 'Nora, don't ever love anyone or anything more than you love God. If you do this, your life will never be completely devastated.' Back then, I'm not sure that I was able to completely understand what she was saying. I was too young perhaps to know the real meaning of faith. But as time went on, I kept her words in mind, and then I understood.

"Toby, everyone's life is full of ups and downs no matter who they are. Some disappointments are much more painful than others. Although your life will change from time to time, as long as you're breathing, God wants you to live as happily as you possibly can. I know that doesn't feel true right now. I know, Toby, believe me I do, but please trust me. It's true. Don't lose your faith for anything.

"Sometimes when people go through hard times, they give up on God because they think God gave up on them, and then they start to think that life owes them something for all their problems, but life doesn't owe us anything.

"My wise son, you'll always have a choice to make. If you choose to love God above all other things, nothing will have the power to completely ruin you. I believe this is one reason Jesus commands us to do this.

"Sometimes, the only way to get back to loving Him or ourselves is to give our love away to someone who can use it even when we feel we don't have any love left in us to give. It's especially when we do this that God returns love to us in abundance.

"Toby, I tell you this because I love you dearly. You must know the truth. The truth is that this won't be the last time someone breaks your heart. It might be your dad again, or another family member, or a friend, or a girlfriend when you're older. I hope this isn't true, but I know better. After all, you can prove this is true yourself because unfortunately, you know this isn't the first time your dad has hurt you. The next time he tells you he's going to show up, or stay longer, or call at a specific time, don't count on it. You can't, Toby. You're too important to always be so disappointed and so sad."

I reminded Toby about how much I loved him, and together, we listed countless other people who were dedicated to looking out for his best. We sat quietly, and he rested against me. He turned to me with tears reforming in his eyes and said, "I wonder if my dad would show up at my funeral if I were dead."

My heart stopped.

My mind raced and searched for the right thing to say.

Finally I spoke. "Well, if you were dead, you wouldn't know if your dad went to your funeral or not."

Toby replied, "Yes I'd know because I'd look down from heaven and see."

"And then what?"

"And then I'd be mad if he didn't go."

"And then what?"

Toby said nothing.

I allowed a few moments of silence to fall between us and hoped he understood.

"Toby, if I ever lost you, I'd cry every second of every minute, of every hour, of every day of the rest of my entire life."

Toby looked at me and told me he loved me, and then he placed his sad head in the crease of his arm.

The next day, I did the only thing I could think to do. I offered Toby new meaning.

CHAPTER 80

When life gives you sour grapes, make snow cones.
—Nora Greyson's journal

In the summertime, when the weather is hot, you
can stretch right up and touch the sky. Have a drink,
have a drive, go out and see what you can find.
—Mungo Jerry

"Grab the sour grape syrup mix, Mommy," Toby told me as he
stood on top of a step stool over a blender that crushed ice, but that
morning, I was too busy dancing to summertime music in our small
kitchen and feeling good. I did a few turn-arounds before tossing
him the cherry flavor syrup mix.

"We're always happy, life's for living, yeah, that's our philosophy,"
I sang in my best Mungo Jerry voice. I was stepping and moving
my head from side to side to the music as I filled a large cooler with
crushed ice.

It did take a village to raise a child. Walking across our front
lawn, she was snapping her fingers playfully above her head and
swaying her hips. "Dee-dee-dee, dee-dee," Leann sang dancing her
way into our kitchen. She winked at Toby and grinned at me before
grabbing the bright yellow table cloth. Singing and swaying, she

walked back outside and unfolded it across the table that sat at the foot of our driveway, fixed it with tape, and attaches a foam board sign in front that read, "Snow Cones Builds Hospital" in large print with pictures of the hospital's progress. "Dee-dah-do, dee-dah-do, dah-do-dah."

The chairs were set behind the table, and a cash box stood ready for filling. Toby's friends arrived just in time as did our first customer.

That day we had wining on our minds!

CHAPTER 81

Gaslighters hover in the lives of kind spirits to see how much manipulation they possess. When we take away their only power, which is our attention to them, we become superior to their process.

—Nora Greyson's journal

Ding. "I love you. I want us back together."

Such messages had been going on for days. The day before, Drew had texted over twenty-four times in fifteen minutes and included downloads of love songs. I ignored every message until the one that read, "Someday, we'll meet again."

Not wanting the responsibility of misinterpreting this message, I responded, "I'm sorry that you're suffering, but I don't feel the same way, and you need to get over this. I will never take you back."

The next day, he was at my front door. "I love you so much. Please give us another chance, Nora. I'd die for you, and you know that."

"If you're not here to talk about setting a visitation schedule to see Toby, I have nothing to say to you, Drew," I said emotionless.

"You can't just throw away sixteen years of marriage. We can't end up apart like this!"

"I have to go. I'll have Toby walk you to your car."

A few moments later, Toby ran up the stairs. "Mommy, guess what? Do you know Daddy's girlfriend Heidi? Daddy just told me she's really nice, and he wants me to meet her, and he's going to marry her! Daddy said you were a loser, Mommy."

Toby told me more about how Drew had described me. It was as if he'd described himself.

CHAPTER 82

Be anxious for nothing, but in everything by prayer
and supplication, with thanksgiving, let your
requests be made known to God; and the peace
of God, which surpasses all understanding, will
guard your hearts and minds through Christ Jesus.
(Philippians 4:6–7 NKJV)

Maintaining a close relationship with God does not guarantee a
perfect life or relief from problems the moment you ask it to, but
it does provide you strength to keep going in the right direction
without getting stuck in the middle. Once you experience God at
a certain level, you want more, and your greatest desire in life is to
protect, bond, nurture, and abide in this relationship.

"I need a break. I need to get away to somewhere peaceful and
decompress. Do you have any suggestions?"

"It's really unfortunate that you have to constantly experience
this. It can be quite exhausting. I do agree that you need a break. I
shall be researching this for you. I know you have been doing your
best, and I've been praying that you don't break down as a result."

"Thank you, Father."

CHAPTER 83

The paradox of life is that it reflects art more often than art reflects life.

—Nora Greyson's diary

A flagstone path led to a wooden bench with a plaque in memory of a beloved Catholic family. Although it was still August, the temperature was pleasant, and nature seeped deep into my soul as the evergreens watched. Split rays of sunlight were cast through the tall oaks and created a dance on the ground below when a friendly breeze passed by. I approached the labyrinth trying to find some spiritual rhythm to release upon. I traced my steps in the circle that led to a stone structure in the center. Resting on one side of its wing was a painted rock that read, Live Happy.

"You must be Nora Greyson." She stretched out her hand to greet mine as I entered the retreat center. "Follow me," Sister Margaret said before guiding me to a small, quiet room where I would stay for the night. Its decorations were restful—white walls, white bedding, a crucifix above a dresser, and a nightstand that included a Bible. Simple and clean, just what my mind and soul were craving. Even the arched willow outside my window seemed more peaceful there than in other parts of the state. I thanked Sister, dropped my overnight bag on the upholstered chair, closed the door, closed the blinds, laid my head on the pillow, lifted my legs onto the mattress, and rested my hands on my stomach. I closed my eyes into a calm spirit.

CHAPTER 84

It is not the strongest of species that survive, nor the most intelligent, but the one most responsive to change.

—Charles Darwin.

Getting an extension of the restraining order took much longer than I had hoped. As a result, I was quite late picking up Toby from summer day camp. I phoned the camp to let them know, but I never mentioned why I would be so late. Without a legitimate excuse, they were understandably annoyed. By the time I arrived, one worker rushed over to me and placed her hands on my arms and asked me if I was okay. Holding her unexpected intensity in, she said, "You're much stronger than you know, and I want you to know everything will be okay. Please stay strong. Please."

I had met this person only a few times during pickup at the end of the day, and we had barely exchanged friendly hellos. I'd never had any other encounters with her. Surprised by her actions, I asked her how she knew. She just nodded. I didn't understand that, but then I looked closer at her face and noticed a long, thin scar that started from her upper left eyebrow, spread diagonally across her cheek, cut through the side of her nose, descended to her lower lip and chin, and ended under her neck right below her earlobe. Perhaps she had had a horrible experience, one that had left her forever vigilant. Perhaps this was God letting me know that I was not alone. I thought both.

CHAPTER 85

No one can make you feel inferior without your consent.

—Eleanor Roosevelt

"Can you tell me the reason you're here today?" a court official asked.

I gave her a brief about my past with Drew.

"How long would you like to extend the restraining order?" she asked.

"As long as I can."

I walked out of her office, and she called Drew in. A few moments later, Drew was released back into the waiting area, and I was called in again.

Her face was as white as the paper she was taking notes on. "Your husband just told me about his twin sister being murdered."

I looked down. "Yes, I'm sure he did. That's the big problem now. I'm in constant fear that he'll try to reenact her death when he's drunk, which is way too frequent. I want some kind of peace of mind so I can sleep for more than two hours a night."

"We can add to the order that he isn't allowed to consume alcohol within twenty-four hours of seeing Toby."

"That sounds like a good addition," I said.

She looked at me with empathy. "Your husband needs help. However, at least for now, he's agreeing to this order."

CHAPTER 86

The Lord watches over the sojourners; he upholds the widow and the fatherless, but the way of the wicked he brings to ruin. (Psalm 146:9 ESV)

December 2019

"Don't give our money away. Nobody will ever help us when we need them to, mark my words."

I recalled Drew saying that to me once when he found me writing a small check to a children's cancer research foundation.

I held my package and walked it to the Christmas tree that was set aside in the front of the church for charities for the homeless. I wondered if Drew would receive it. Maybe I should have just personally given the package to him myself since he claimed to have been sleeping in his car in different parking lots since the previous week.

I was again getting at least twenty texts from him twice a week if not more saying he loved and missed me. I didn't respond. I didn't think he realized that the restraining order was still in effect and it was a felony per text message.

We had recently returned to court for nonpayment of child

support. Following the court date, Drew was able to come up with $600 for a back child support payment. He must have been getting money from somewhere. And why should I have believed that he was really homeless? If that were true, I'd never have wished it on him.

This divorce was to be finalized within a month, but that didn't seem soon enough.

CHAPTER 87

Jesus looked at him and said, "How hard it is for the rich to enter the kingdom of God! Indeed, it is easier for a camel to go through the eye of a needle than for someone who is rich to enter the kingdom of God." (Luke 18:24–29 NIV)

"Mommy, if you could have anything in the world, what would it be?" Toby asked.

"I would have a completely united and loving family."

"I'm kind of getting used to the way things are now. If I could have anything in the world, it would be to have a lot of money, Mommy."

I grinned as I glanced over the picnic table at him. "I'm glad you're not as sad today as you have been."

Toby sat in his black, faux-fur-lined hoodie zipped up to his chin and was holding a bag of popcorn and looking across the ocean. A seagull landed nearby and squawked at the smell of the fresh kernels.

"Throughout life, you'll hear people say that money is the root of all evil. That simply isn't true, and it's the most misused verse in the Bible. Money itself isn't evil. In fact, it's necessary for survival. In addition, it can bring a certain level of happiness to our lives. It's when we love money more than we love people that it becomes evil.

It's when people are filled with so much pride and fear that they cannot let a penny of their money go to help someone else and they become obsessed with worldly possessions. St. Francis of Assisi says, 'Riches prick us with a thousand troubles in getting them, as many cares in preserving them, and yet more anxiety in spending them, and with grief in losing them.'"

"But I like buying things, Mommy."

"Oh yes, so do I, and I believe it's okay to buy nice things for ourselves once in a while, and I believe God wants us to. He just doesn't want us to be greedy or be controlled by money. He'll notice even in your most fearful days of survival if you give a little to someone less fortunate than you. That said, choose to give anyway, but be wise. God would not want you to suffer a lost meal.

"Toby, when I look back at the times in my life and compare how I felt after spending too much money on myself to the feeling I had when I was charitable, there's no doubt which time provided me greater joy and satisfaction. Being charitable and especially with your heart is one way of knowing what it's like to feel God's kingdom on earth because God is Love in a full circle. In other words, God is generous with us because He loves us completely, so we should show our gratitude to Him by being generous with love toward others. That way, His circle isn't interrupted. St. Francis of Assisi also said, 'The rich man who gives to the poor does not bestow alms but pays a debt.' Some of these things you may need to be a little older to fully understand, but that's okay," I explained as I threw a Frisbee to Toby standing on top of seashells.

I was grateful that God granted me these moments and wisdom to teach our son His important lessons. I just hoped I was doing it the right way.

CHAPTER 88

God grant me the serenity to accept the things I cannot change, courage to change the things I can and wisdom to know the difference.

—Reinhold Niebuhr

January 2020

Sometimes, taking it one day at a time is too much. One moment at a time might be more bearable.

It had been over a year since Drew had left, and I was frustrated to admit that I'd been dealing with another seesaw bout of emotions. I'd cried for days but didn't know why. I felt ashamed because of all that Drew had put Toby and me through. I should have been glad that he was gone. But in my mind, Drew hadn't left. He had died. I didn't know this person called Drew anymore. Only God could help him.

At one time, Drew had a real love for his family. There were defects as there are in all relationships, but the love we shared was real and deeply imbedded for a very long time. As hard as it was to convince new friends of the wonderful father and husband Drew used to be, it was even harder to convince old friends that he wasn't anymore. Each time, it cut deep with disbelief as I listened to the same words: "I don't care who Drew's having an affair with. There's no way he loves anyone more than he loves you. He'd follow you to the end of this world," they'd testify.

Some people thought that Drew had left me for another woman. He hadn't. He'd allowed his weaknesses to overpower his morals for a momentary ego boost, and then his life spiraled out of control to the point that he was convinced that he could never return to himself. As the devil's usual course of temptation went, *It's just one time* had been whispered to Drew during a frail moment, and he had fallen for it. And one time turned into two and two turned into a change of identity.

When I looked back and removed the emotions from all the situations and just examined the facts, I realized that Drew had actually admitted exactly when he had had his first affair. When I had reflected previously, I had noticed only his change in appearance and demeanor that occurred after his first arrest. But what I had missed were his words: "I don't need you. I could walk away and never come back," he had said. I had been too quick to dismiss that maybe because I thought he was saying it in the heat of an argument and didn't mean it. But I came to realize what he was really saying was that he was having an affair and I had become at least sexually replaceable.

Yesterday, he texted me sixty-seven times about how much he regretted his decision. I didn't respond to any of his messages.

CHAPTER 89

It's better to stomp on those eggshells than to tiptoe around them. The beauty of broken eggshells is that they lay out a pathway to freedom.

—Nora Greyson's journal

February 2020

Toby and I were making homemade pasta and listening to Italian music while pretending we were traveling through Italy when suddenly Drew stumbled through the back door and onto our kitchen floor smiling and stretching his hand out holding a child support payment. He approached me as if I should have been expecting him prepared with a prize for his good deed.

He was barefoot even though it was 16 degrees outside. His blond hair and unruly beard were bushy and wild. His cheap sweatpants were torn, and his old, ragged leather jacket seemed to have a hard time covering his continuously growing and bloated body. He was a far cry from the husband I used to know.

I jumped and spun around startled by his arrival. Toby ran up to him and gave him a big hug. "Daddy! You're here!"

Ignoring Toby, Drew stood inches from me. "Put your hands out," he said as he wobbled smiling.

"No," I replied.

"Touch my hands," he said as he held his palms up and continued to stretch them toward me.

"No. You need to leave, Drew," I said wide eyed still in disbelief that he was in my kitchen just inches from me. Instead of leaving, he sat at the table as if he had never moved out and hadn't been sporadically missing for the past year. He began to tell me about his new job.

"I just bought some boneless chicken for a dollar eighty-nine a pound," he said as if he'd just returned from grocery shopping for our family as he used to.

Why in the world would a homeless person buy raw boneless chicken? Where does he plan on cooking it? "Drew, you can't just walk into this house unexpectedly."

"Where do you live, Daddy?"

"Good news is that I'm parked nearby now, and I can visit more often."

"Toby, please go in your room so your dad and I can have adult talk time," I said.

I tilted my head slightly and glared at Drew in disapproval because he'd just let Toby know that he was homeless, but he didn't catch on to my body language. Instead, he offered a childlike smile and looked at me as though I were supposed to be happy about this information.

I regretted not locking the door after walking Olive. I also regretted blocking Drew from my phone. Maybe if I hadn't blocked him, I would have received a warning about his arrival. I thought back to the night that Amie was murdered and wondered if things would have turned out differently if she hadn't blocked Seth though by no means had her death been any fault of hers. Calling this a difficult determination was by far an understatement.

From the corner of my eye, I spotted Toby.

"Mommy, please let me talk to Daddy before he leaves."

As difficult as it was to put aside my motherly protective instincts, I granted Toby's request.

CHAPTER 90

Within an inflexible mind lies a future told by its
past, and the wise words of courageous Toby.
—Nora Greyson's journal

Toby walked cautiously to his dad, sat beside him in silence, and tenderly placed his hand over his father's hand.

"Toby, I love you with all my heart," Drew said. "I still protect you and your mother with my life, and I always will. Just because your mother and I aren't together anymore doesn't mean I don't care. I failed, Toby, but I never wanted to. Don't ever make the same mistake I made."

Toby's gazed compassionately at his father. "Dad, if the decisions you've made are bothering you, you should confess them to God. I love you too, and I know what I'm talking about. Even if no one else forgives you, God can forgive you, and it will all be forgotten. I just want you to be better."

"I wish God was here," Drew said with his head hung low.

"God *is* here, Daddy. I know this may sound creepy but God is actually listening to us right now. Even if you don't feel Him, He never leaves."

"Toby, I have a lot of making up to do with your mom. I need to get back into your lives and stay there forever. This was all my fault, and I regret it severely."

I almost intervened, but then I remembered how Drew had left. There had been no goodbye, no emotional exchange between father and son, no reliable visitation schedule, and no explanation or assurance offered to Toby at all. Even though it was clear that Drew was trying to gain his son's pity, at least he was finally apologizing, and I let Toby absorb it all. Toby deserved to hear that he had done absolutely nothing wrong straight from his father's mouth.

"Even if you are to do that, you still need to start by talking to God and getting a therapist. If you did something really bad like declined God's love, that's why you feel empty, Dad."

"I'll talk to God. I want to make things right, and that's the bottom line, but I can't afford a therapist. I want you to know though that I never put you last, Toby."

"Maybe you should tell God that you want to make things right so He can give you ideas on how to do that. And then maybe you can do things with me again like you used to. I think if you stop drinking every day, you'll have a clearer mind and make better decisions. You can get sick living this way, and you should take care of yourself mentally and physically.

"I know you've heard me say this a bunch of times already, but I'll say it a million more. I want you to be the best person you can be, Dad. There's still hope, and it's never too late to change. Your life isn't over. If you love me, you have to hear me."

Toby spoke with such a pure quality of innocence and truth; it was enough to convert any open-minded sinner into an instant saint. "Also, Dad, God can tell if you're lying or not."

"You're right, Toby. I need a lot of help. Everything turned into a mess. You're a better man than I am. This is not something I want you to worry about. All this is killing me, and I love you and miss you so much. I'll never let you down. How can I make this right?"

"But Dad, you have let me down. When you left me, that was the most hurtful thing ever. What's your plan to make everything right? You should start off small. When you start off with small things, they become big in the end. Maybe you can go back to school. A lot of adults go back to school."

"I can't believe my son is advising me like this." Drew put his hand on Toby's back. "I really admire the way you speak so intelligently, and I love you so much. Why don't we all start new? Let's talk to Mommy and see what she thinks. I wish I was a better person. I don't even know where I'm living from one day to the next. I'm willing to go through any kind of scrutiny to make this right. I just miss all of us. You are my son, the love of my life, and I'll always take care of you."

Toby frowned. "Dad, if you say you want to be better, than act like it. I know the truth hurts, but you have to hear it. You don't even visit me anymore. You barely even call."

"Yeah, I hate myself every day of my life because of that."

"Stop hating yourself, and ask God to help you. Every answer you're looking for, even if you don't know it, God does, so you will eventually have it. And start doing nice things for other people."

"I'm going to make the right choices and do the right things. It's been awful, but I promise you, Toby, I'll do nice things for you."

"Yeah, but is it just for me or for other people too?" Toby asked.

"No, I don't care about other people. Just you, Mommy, and me."

"You shouldn't be like that, Dad. Even though you got lost, that doesn't mean you should be like that. There are people out there who need things, and you could be useful to them. You should care about them. That's what nice people do. They don't care just about specific people."

"Yeah, well, if I saw someone who needed help, I'd help them. That's just human nature. But as far as my feelings, my roots are in this house, and I have to get back here and make everything right."

"Dad, it's getting late. I have to go to bed now."

"Okay. You have no idea how good it was to talk to you like this. Can I call you tomorrow morning?"

"Yeah, Dad. I want you to start calling me every day. Because you still feel down, but at least that will make you feel a little better."

"Toby, I promise I'll start calling you every single day. I love you. Goodnight."

"I love you too, Dad." Toby hugged his father goodnight.

Toby sounded like a little professional. He stood with hope knowing he loved as deeply as his soul was anchored to the pit of this earth, and he walked away with satisfaction and integrity. Drew couldn't have received better advice if he'd paid for it.

After Toby left the room, I had to ask Drew to leave several times before he did.

Even though Drew promised, the next morning there was no phone call. When Toby reached Drew that evening, he apologized and asked to see Toby the following Thursday. The following Thursday came and went, and Drew never showed up, but I'd known that he wouldn't, and I'd prepared Toby the best I could for the disappointment.

"I'm too embarrassed to be seen looking like this. I feel like a disgusting mess," Drew said to me.

I said nothing.

When Toby started talking, he didn't hold back a single expression of disappointment. Drew apologized extensively pleading with Toby to give him another chance. "I promise I'll see you Sunday."

Sunday came, and Drew said he wasn't able to take a shower and couldn't make it. That time, Toby screamed at his dad, "All you ever do is break my heart! I never want to see you again!"

On his knees, face flushed with anger, fists pressed against the floor, he exploded with heavy grunts that erupted between forced shut teeth.

I got down on the ground and held him. "Toby, I'm so proud of all the advice and wisdom you offered your dad, but you aren't the adult in this relationship. Whether he realizes it or not he makes you feel sorry for him and think that there's something you could do to help him, but that's wrong. The truth is that until he wants to help himself, he'll be just like he is now regardless of what you or anyone else says or does, and right now he isn't capable of making good decisions. He's very confused and has lost his sense of knowing how to be a good dad. The only benefit you'll receive by continuing to speak to him under these circumstances is a temporary satisfaction that you at least heard his voice, and even at that, it's a voice that will leave you feeling sad and frustrated."

"Words can be nice to hear, but if they aren't put into action, they aren't sincere. We have to learn to judge people by what they do, not by what they say they'll do. I'm sorry, Toby. I'm glad you had the courage to express your disappointment and anger toward your dad today. It was well overdue."

Knowing the debilitating effects of fatherlessness, I hated my words as they left my mouth, but I couldn't allow this to stay open to Toby's interpretation.

As I held him, I wondered if I had done the right thing by allowing this to happen. I wondered how much he truly understood and could be beneficial to his emotional evolvement. As much as I wanted to protect Toby from the negative actions of his father, I knew in my heart that if I forced his dad out of his life, he would grow up holding onto false hope because he would have me to question for keeping his father away. Right or wrong, it was not my truth to tell.

PART VII

TABULA RASA

Then the delight, when your courage kindled, and out you stepped onto new ground, your eyes young again with energy and dream, a path of plenitude opening before you.

Though your destination is not yet clear you can trust the promise of this opening; unfurl yourself into the grace of beginning that is at one with your life's desire.

—John O'Donohue

CHAPTER 91

He who blames others has a long way to go on his journey. He who blames himself is halfway there. He who blames no one has arrived.

—Chinese proverb

March 2020

My divorce had been finalized, and what had once seemed a hopeless financial situation had been turned around. Drew agreed to pay weekly child support and even weekly alimony, something my lawyer and I had thought impossible. Although I was fully aware that you couldn't get blood from a stone, at least this was legally documented.

As we were sworn in, the judge still held the right to override Drew's decision especially because of the low income he was claiming. He asked Drew several times if he agreed to these terms though he had already signed the paperwork. Drew replied yes. Our financial settlement was honored. In addition, I was granted full sole and legal custody of Toby.

God is righteous. He brings justice to the unjust, comforts the brokenhearted, and clears a new path for His believers.

After I left the courthouse, I went for a long walk at a beach, took deep breaths, and thanked God for everything.

Eighteen years of Drew's strong, gentle embrace, my hand in his hand both pressed tenderly against his heart. The smooth shave of his soft skin and fresh scent of his cologne rest on top of my head that rests against his chest, and we slowly dance to the music that played in our kitchen.

This dance appears before me now, and gradually, Drew is gone from the scene. As my feet twirl gracefully over new ground, my dress lifts in fullness and my hands reach freely toward the sky.

The sky is not my limit. It's just a stepping stone.

I rest back on high rocks that cantilever over the waves and close my eyes. I imagine a lingering daytime moon that softens the hem of a cool morning sky, where wild horses run in freedom sands, a place my thoughts never used to wander.

My boots stretch out at this final goodbye, past the seashells, past a thousand pages of my mind where I leave Drew as he once left me—so very far behind.

I forgive you, Drew.

CHAPTER 92

We ought always to thank God for you, brothers
and sisters, and rightly so, because your faith is
growing more and more, and the love you all have
for one another is increasing. (2 Thessalonians
1:3 NIV)

There are four general and unique categories of love. *Eros* is romantic
love, *storge* is family love, *philia* is brotherly love that unites believers
of Christ, and *agape* is God's divine love for humankind, the
strongest of all love. It is unconditional, sacrificial, immeasurable,
unchanging, and pure. It is perfect and flawless.

> Whatsoever you do to the least of my brothers
> That you do unto Me!
> When I was hungry you gave me to eat.
> When I was thirsty you gave me to drink.
> Now enter into the home of your Father.
> —Willard F. Jabusch

Six hundred dollars. That's all it took to provide an education,
books, a uniform, and two meals a day for one child for an entire
year in Nigeria. I was ashamed to admit that Drew and I used to

easily spend that amount on Toby for Christmas and then complain that he had too many toys.

I didn't really know what to expect since this was my first time doing this, but with every donation, the joy of my excitement was reignited. It's incredible how happy it made me to have come up with the full amount especially because of my lack of involvement in social media fundraising.

Father had just returned from his annual three-week journey to Nigeria, and I had never seen him so happy. I can only compare his bliss to that of a mother who had just given birth to her firstborn because in a sense, he in fact gave birth to many lives by means of rescue.

The hospital was about 75 percent complete. Orphans sang to him in praises to God, and a young widow of five finally had a roof that connected the walls of her home to protect her and her children from the harsh environment.

> When I was tired you helped me find rest.
> When I was worried you calmed all my fears.
> Now enter the home of your Father.
> —Willard F. Jabusch

CHAPTER 93

You have not lived today until you have done
something for someone who can never repay you.
—John Bunyan.

"Father, I have only one request. I'd like for the child I sponsor to be older. It seems most people want to sponsor a young child, and I'm sure they have their reasons, but I have mine. I can only imagine the devastating feeling of lost hope an older child must feel every single time a cute young one is chosen before them," I said.

I know what it's like to feel time has sucked you up into a capsule that no one wants to look at anymore, I thought miserably.

Father showed me a video of him interviewing several kids in need of support. It was eighteen minutes long.

"I can't do this. There are too many children. You decide," I said.

"Are you sure?" he asked.

"Yes."

"Okay. I shall be thinking about your request."

"Thank you, Father," I said relieved.

CHAPTER 94

God blessed me with joy by giving me Joy.
—Nora Greyson's journal

"How'd you decide, Father?" I asked.

"She touched my heart. I really felt for her. Like many children, Joy is sent to a public school, which means she is sent somewhere to sit in dirt every day and hope that a teacher will stop by for ten minutes a week. When she returns home after her so-called school day, she has to go into the forest to try to find whatever she can to turn into something worth selling so she can feed her four younger siblings. This is her everyday life."

"How old is she?"

"Eleven."

I paused a moment to watch a video of Father trying to find a sponsor for her. I never realized a heart could break the way mine did that day. "What about her mother?"

"Her mother's elderly. Late forties is considered elderly in that part of Nigeria. There's no medical care. Her mother isn't able to help that much, Nora."

"And her father?"

"Please understand, Nora. It's not like here. Many poor families travel up northern Nigeria in hope of finding work. If a terrorist realizes that the man of the family is Christian and won't convert to his faith, he murders that man usually right in front of his wife and children. To answer your question, Joy doesn't even remember meeting her father. After a widow returns to her village, she's cut off from all means of survival because women are considered worthless without husbands, and many times, she dies in despair, one reason there are so many orphans."

Read that again.

CHAPTER 95

You are not a drop in the ocean. You are an entire
ocean in a drop.

—Rumi

April 2020

After ten years, today was the last day at my place of employment
with a small graphic design company. The COVID-19 virus was
spreading throughout the world claiming many lives already,
and we were only at the beginning of what people were calling
a pandemic. Because of its extreme contagiousness and ability to
kill, especially the vulnerable elderly and people with compromised
immune systems, schools had shut down, churches had closed, and
numerous businesses had been subjected to mandatory shutdowns.
In some areas, entire states with the exception of grocery stores, gas
stations, hospitals and a few other essential businesses had become
unavailable to the public.

Once again, I was filled with mixed emotions due to being
unemployed and finally having a break to heal from my losses.
Looking at my finances, I couldn't see any way I could keep my
house. It hadn't been even a full month since my divorce, and that
eliminated the opportunity to see a complete billing cycle of how

my money could cover my living expenses. In a few days, we would be joining in the state shutdowns, removing any possibility for me to even look for a job.

As people hoarded in fear, grocery store shelves were depleted of produce, canned goods, meat, and dairy and completely emptied in other areas such as paper supplies especially toilet paper, which has become more worthy than gold. In addition, there was absolutely no hand sanitizer available in any store or online. Leanne phoned me saying she didn't have any hand sanitizer; she had received the news one day late that a shortage would soon take place. Knowing there wouldn't be any sanitizers at the larger stores, I went to a body shop hoping they might have some pocket sanitizers, but when I arrived, there was a sign on the door saying, "Sorry, we are out of hand sanitizer." I couldn't find even bleach or rubbing alcohol to make my own. I thought, *Okay, God, I guess finding hand sanitizer is out of the question*, and then I continued with my errands, which included grocery shopping and going to the bank.

When I arrived at the bank, after making my transaction, the teller handed me something. I had Toby with me, so I assumed it was some sort of candy. I thanked her for the gift and asked what was in the little black case. She smiled and said, "Hand sanitizer."

"Thank you so much!" Only slightly exaggerating, I added, "Did you know this is probably worth a small fortune right now?"

Still smiling, she said, "You're welcome."

"I really am so grateful to be receiving this from you. My elderly friend just realized the seriousness of frequent sanitizing right now with the scare of this spreading virus, and I'm glad I'll be able to give this to her. Thank you so much!"

The teller then handed me a second bottle of sanitizer. I couldn't believe it! It felt like she kept handing me precious gems that was untold to the rest of the human population.

I thought, *If God can provide me with hand sanitizer when it's impossible to find, I have no doubt He can provide for me financially even though I have no idea how. Faith over fear. God, I trust You.* And then my soul was calm and even joyful regardless of how unfeasible things appeared through my own logical belief system.

During this trying time in my life, I grew accustomed to recognizing that parallel to God lurks the Prince of Darkness patiently waiting for me to feel defeated and anxious and for me to question why God hasn't protected me from so many losses. But I don't feel this way. Instead, I feel closer to God than ever especially with the understanding that most of my losses were due to other people's poor choices. God assures me that He is with me.

And the peace of God, which surpasses all understanding, will guard your hearts and your minds in Christ Jesus. (Philippians 4:7 ESV)

I have had many moments of doubt and depression, which go hand in hand. I am not super strong spiritually; I fall, and sometimes, I stay down for a long time, so long that the familiarity of misery creates an illusion of being more comfortable than the effort it takes to realize something better could be near.

Realize hope.

God is very patient and forgiving indeed, and if we don't give up on Him, He won't give up on us. That I will put in writing as a promise.

CHAPTER 96

Personalities form from the emotions of our trauma, regardless if the trauma is minor or substantial. The good news is that these personalities can be reshaped. When we face our pain, we could and should allow its meaning to change so we do not become locked in a state of being a victim of our trauma but instead purposely take one step at a time into a desired future self for the sake of allowing our trauma to become a benefit to our lives. During this fragile stage, choosing the right empathetic listener is essential to achieving the desired outcome.

—Nora Greyson's journal

Although a calling is known to show itself in many ways, the most unlikely form is God suddenly appearing in front of you dressed in a white robe telling you what He wants you to do with your life. My definition of that kind of experience would be a hallucination. A calling in most cases is a deeply implanted divine seed that emanates from our consciousness and becomes an all-knowing invitation to be at one with God, to glorify Him, seek His will, and show the mercy and wisdom we receive from Him to others as He has called us to do so. It is an exceptional honor to realize because it means God truly trusts us to accomplish what He has planned through us.

The assignment is of this mountain. The purpose is to prove it can be moved. The thrill is unshakable no matter what, but don't be misled by these words. God does not call us to be His prisoners. Just the opposite is true, and nothing else feels as joyfully satisfying as trying to achieve this goal.

"Father, I can't help this feeling I've had during the past few years, even before my ex left us," I said.

"What is it?"

"I feel I'm supposed to help fatherless children. I just don't know how I'm supposed to do that. After all, I'm not a father. I have no formal education in that area, just some personal experiences, a little bit of research, and some evaluations. But at the same time, this is all I think about, and it won't let me rest, nor do I want it to. It's exciting and frustrating because I don't even know where to begin. I often wonder how these helpless children process statistical information. I can only imagine their sense of a doomed future in addition to the heartbreak that has been forced into their lives by the rejection of their fathers. They need to know they are not just numbers. They are human beings, and I refuse to stand by and not say anything especially since this has been sewn into my soul. I need to somehow figure out a way to be the difference for them."

"Nora, you do know that I counsel married couples and I'm very good at it, yet I never had any personal experiences with being in this type of a relationship."

He had a good point. *God, if this is Your will for my life, please bring me the right people to work with. Show me the way, and let it be done.*

> With man this is impossible, but with God all
> things are possible. (Matthew 19:26 NIV)

CHAPTER 97

Enter into the promises of God. It is your inheritance. You will do more in one year if you are really filled with the Holy Ghost than you could do in fifty years apart from Him.

—Smith Wigglesworth

I can't sleep. I'm getting used to the idea of a slower-paced world, and I like it. My mind is full of gratitude and wonder. It's a tabula rasa, a clean slate.

I have considered my quarantined bucket list, and it goes something like this.

1. Spend quality time with Toby and Olive.
2. Rest. Lord knows I need it.
3. Pray, pray, and pray some more. Lord knows I need that too.
4. Create some new pieces of art.
5. Attend weekday Mass at least one day a week in addition to Sundays.
6. Catch up on some books I haven't had time to read.
7. Learn a new language.
8. Explore the idea of falling in love with someone new.
9. Look into new investments.

10. Make assessments of my physical being, and change areas that could use improvement if possible. If nothing else, I'll treat myself by getting some new clothes if financially feasible.

11. Meet my favorite author. This may be impossible since traveling is a huge health risk right now, and I'm sure no book signings are taking place during this pandemic shutdown.

12. Turn these journals into a book and publish it.

CHAPTER 98

The secret of change is to focus all of your energy,
not of fighting the old, but on building the new.
                                                    —Socrates

During this year's Lenten season, I know exactly what I was fasting from—TV, social media, and all the other useless noise that consumed my time and didn't apply to my situation anyway.

As a rule of thumb, when I present design choices to my clients, I limit them to three of the best according to their needs and desires. This simplifies things and simple sounds really good, so I'm implementing this rule in my personal life. Three ways of useful entertainment; anything more will just be a mental distraction.

I will consider this time as a gift to clean out my mind, my heart, and oh yes, all that stuff around my house that is causing me to feel guilty knowing that it used to be money. And I will give my mind, heart, and all that stuff to people who can benefit from it. I will recreate my home into an environment that will help me remember who I want to become instead of what has happened to me.

Oh, and that pipe that broke in my house last year during Easter weekend just so happened to grant me the financial ability to replace my kitchen, which had imprisoned me with so many debilitating memories. Hallelujah!

When this phrase is through, I hope to provide a fresh foundation for God to work from, and then I will get out of His way and be patient. I have evolved enough to understand that waiting on God doesn't mean complaining every five minutes that my prayers haven't been answered yet but instead having confidence in His perfect timing and appreciate every flower, smile, and moments that are symbols of love and hope along the way while He creates a new path for me.

CHAPTER 99

He makes me to lie down in green pastures; He leads me beside the still waters. He restores my soul; He leads me in the paths of righteousness For His names sake. Yea, though I walk through the valley of the shadow of death, I will fear no evil; for You are with me; Your rod and Your staff, they comfort me. You prepare a table before me in the presence of my enemies; You anoint my head with oil; my cup runs over. Surely goodness and mercy shall follow me all the days of my life; and I will dwell in the house of the Lord Forever. (Psalm 23:2–6 NKJV)

June 2020

Bike rides are long against warm daytime breezes, and hikes through the forest have more time, but the one who was most happy about all this staying home business was Olive.

The government was pressuring all to quarantine themselves in an attempt to achieve some control and safety from this virus. I left my house only about twice a month for necessities, and I had plenty of items stocked up in my basement. There were very few cars on the road, and wearing a mask had become a government mandate everywhere in public.

Outside of homeschooling, Toby learned how to mow the lawn, stain the deck, paint the front porch, repair a loose step, sew a button on his shirt, and bake homemade bread. The greatest of all is that he and Olive became quite the movie clip stars as they continued to raise money by means of a virtual snow cone stand that realized over $220 for the continued construction of the hospital in Nigeria. Not bad considering one would have to use his imagination to receive the treat.

I ordered new cabinets for my kitchen and planned the start date in August to mark something positive on my sister-in-law's birthday and the anniversary of the day I was first physically abused. I painted most of the interior of my house, repaired a few pieces of siding, and cleaned out my closets, the basement, and the filing cabinet out from which crawled over a decade and a half of joint tax returns. *Yikes!*

I caught up on some reading, completed a few new pieces of art work, studied French on audio books, and dated someone who loved buying me clothes. Although the relationship was short lived, I was glad for the experience, and I later accepted it as a two-in-one check off on my quarantine bucket list. And I met my favorite author at an open zoom meeting. I didn't think that one would be possible even though I should have known better by this time.

Mortgage payments had been deferred, and unemployment benefits were granted with the application for job searches waived. Government stimulus checks were compensating in a financial sense for the lack of child support alleviating a financial burden. All that was left to do was breathe.

And whenever we felt like it, we drove off to open fields or the ocean, and I watched Toby and Olive run freely and play.

CHAPTER 100

Too many times, we leave what is good to search for who we are, instead of staying in the comfort of good and evolving into someone we aspire to become.

—Nora Greyson's journal

July 2020

Dew was still living in his car with no air-conditioning, and the summer heat was hovering around 96. Due to COVID-19, public showers had been closed. He hadn't been able to find work because he had no address to put on job applications, and he had been eating loaves of day-old bread he got from a food pantry. He refilled his water bottles in public bathroom sinks, and he had an unexplained and excessively swollen foot.

He claimed to have phone service only for calls and texts. He told me that all his belongings were sitting in stomach-turning filth in the trunk of his once-beautiful car that was covered in dirt, scratches, and dents and with a decaying engine due to lack of maintenance.

It had been almost six months since Drew last saw Toby.

I attempted again to speak to him about turning to God, about forgiveness, and how he could learn to forgive himself. I offered to research shelters, and I gave him permission to use my address on job applications. He sounded appreciative. Through his tears and shame, he apologized for all he had done. As heartbreaking as it was to hear, I kept my side of the conversation businesslike. I didn't want him to get emotionally attached, yet my conscience wouldn't allow me to ignore the pity I felt for him.

I provided him with information about a place that ran a program to help alcoholics and a list of homeless shelters even though due to the raging numbers of people catching the virus there was a long waiting list.

He thanked me extensively.

I didn't respond.

CHAPTER 101

Negative people will create new problems whenever they are given new solutions.

—Nora Greyson's journal

Jeremiah was a bullfrog. Was a good friend of mine.
I never understood a single word he said,
but I helped him a-drink his wine,
and he always had some mighty fine wine.
Singin' joy to the world.

—Three Dog Night

Toby and I were admiring our beautiful, newly remodeled kitchen. The insurance company had replaced everything that had been damaged. What once seemed an addition to a pile of overflowing and unbearable troubles had turned into a welcoming breath of fresh air, and I thanked God that I'd never given up.

"Your turn, Mom," Toby said.

"No way. There's no good one to pull," I replied.

Toby laughed. "I know ... but it's your turn."

Ding.

I pulled the third one in from the second to bottom row. I held my breath—*Easy now.* "Yes!" I shouted as I realized the tower hadn't dropped.

Ding.

"My turn," Toby said and poked slightly at a wooden piece. I was suddenly jealous that his fingers were smaller than mine. From the opposite side, he gave a gentle tug. Our bodies stiffened. Olive glanced up with as much concern as a pup could offer. We wondered if Toby could do it.

One minute passed.

"Nope," Toby's voice quivered and he pushed the halfway pulled out block back into the tower. He tried another. He nudged it just a little at a time.

Ding.

Anticipation filled the air. Steady as a crossbow aiming at a bull's-eye, his grasp gave a final pull. And then we exhaled.

Ding.

It was my turn, but again, I couldn't find any good place to draw from.

Ding.

I finally glanced at my phone while Toby stood and spun with Olive and sang Three Dog Night's "If I were the king of the world, tell you what I'd do …"

Drew had texted over sixty times in less than forty-five minutes about how much he loved and missed me. *No good deed goes unpunished*, I thought as I reflected on the previous day's conversation. I locked my doors and windows, kept a close eye on my phone for any clues that he might be in the area, notified the neighbors to be on the lookout, and pulled another block.

PART VIII

IT IS WELL WITH MY SOUL

My grace is sufficient for you, for my power is made perfect in weakness. Therefore I will boast all the more gladly about my weaknesses, so that Christ's power may rest on me. That is why, for Christ's sake, I delight in weaknesses, in insults, in hardships, in persecutions, in difficulties. For when I am weak, then I am strong. (Corinthians 12:9–10 NIV)

CHAPTER 102

October 2020

"In the name of the Father, and of the Son and of the Holy Spirit, amen. I will praise Your grace of Fire, and I will celebrate this inheritance so the gift of time may never again be wasted, not even in my darkest hour. With confidence, I know You always have been and forever will be with me. I pray that You might grant me fortitude, wisdom, patience, and compassion as I release my pride before You in the hope that Thy will to be done."

Soft light illuminated enormous stained-glass windows in a place where stillness rested on a crucifix above the altar. Like Veronica during the Passion of Christ, I was moved by the sight of Him carrying His heavy cross with extreme exhaustion and unbearable pain due to betrayal. And also like Veronica, I offered my veil. On it, the image of His face remained, and in the shadow of His wings, I rejoiced.

As I sat in the pew, I stared at Jesus on the cross and watched His stillness evolve. I saw Him suffering in humiliation alone. And then I saw Him at peaceful rest and with many—with me. As much as the foundation of His love remained unchanged, His care for the forgiveness of our sins far exceeded beyond anything we can imagine as humans. Through the acknowledgement of His sacrifice we can find the desire to love others as we are called to love ourselves with kindness. There was a separate type of peace that I'd found while sitting in a quiet church before weekday Mass that I never experienced during Sunday service."I do not wish to sit here as a hypocrite but to admit that I am very far from perfect, and only Your grace God can help me. Regretfully, the truth that I think I desire Your will does not mean that I am always doing it, but I believe my desire does please you. My faults I repent, and I ask for Your forgiveness and mercy because I do not want to be separated from You, nor will I boast in creditability for any moments that I may have in the past or may become in the future a blessing to someone else's life. This is Your work in sending the Holy Spirit to dwell in me. All honor, all praise and all glory is Yours forever and ever, amen."

It always amazed me and in a shameful way the temptation I felt to do anything but go to church again during a following weekday especially when I was always glad to be there once I was there. There's a remarkable difference in the remaining parts of my days that start with prayer and the days that do not.

When all the world is still, that is the peace of God in His holy, mighty power and gift to us.

In your eyes, the light, the heat; in your eyes I am complete; in your eyes I see the doorway to a thousand churches; in your eyes the resolution of all the fruitless searches. I wanna touch the light the heat I see in your eyes.

Peter Gabriel, "In Your Eyes"

CHAPTER 103

For you created my inmost being; you knit me together in my mother's womb. I praise you because I am fearfully and wonderfully made; your works are wonderful, I know that full well. My frame was not hidden from you when I was made in the secret place, when I was woven together in the depths of the earth. Your eyes saw my unformed body; all the days ordained for me were written in your book before one of them came to be. (Psalm 139:13–16 NIV)

November 2020

God is the photosynthesis of life. He is the beginning and the end, the complete circle of Love, and the complete circle of Life. All is brought to life by Him and returned to Him; there's no escaping it.

When God tells us we are marvelously made with the thought of His Son Jesus in mind, He means it literally. Cells hold our skin on and our organs together with a glue-like protein molecule called laminin, which according to research is cross-like in shape.

Since we are all made equally in His image, I don't believe for a second that God loves me any more than He loves Drew or anyone else. The difference in the outcome of our lives is usually or at least in some part our choice if nothing else but by way of perception.

Just as water can be used to quench our thirst or drown us, our free will can be used to do good or evil; it is entirely up to us, but in the end, I don't believe God will be interested in our opinions about other people's lives. I believe He will be alone with us to judge us individually on how we have chosen to use our free will. How well have we lived? How well have we loved? They are the same.

The most common thing people wish they had more of at the end of their lives is time, yet how much time do we waste trying to impress people we don't even like? It's a thief defined as pride, and its price is extremely expensive. Meanwhile, as we sulk, we tell our loved ones we are too busy to be with them, but if we are honest, we will admit that our self-pity and pride take priority over spending time with them. Only then can we start to understand how we are making them feel. If we're not careful, wasted time can erase all the remaining days of our lives. All of them.

Perhaps a good antidote is to schedule regular appointments with God and think about death. Yes, death, because sometimes, that's the only way to get back to life. It's good and healthy to evaluate our mortality from time to time and ask ourselves, if today was the last day of our lives, would we be happy looking back on our choices?

Purposely think about your thoughts and especially when you're feeling overwhelmed and defeated. How are they affecting your present, your future, and your past? If you can't control your situation, give it to God; otherwise, you will surely spin yourself into frustrating, useless circles trying to become Him.

The reason some of us are uncomfortable with our final days is because of regret, yet it seems that God gives us sufficient time. Thank God that you are among the fortunate to have been woken up this morning by doing something good about it.

Today is Thanksgiving Day. It is the anniversary of when Drew and my eighteen-year relationship started and ended—the full circle.

It has been two years to date since he left us, and since then, he has slowly and regretfully disappeared from our lives and into a dark, lonely pit of pride and shame, but I refuse to give up on praying for him. He didn't destroy my life. I won't allow him that kind of emotional power over me. But unfortunately, he did destroy his own life by his poor decisions.

CHAPTER 104

Eternal God, in whom mercy is endless and the treasury of compassion inexhaustible, look kindly upon us and increase Your mercy in us, that in difficult moments we might not despair nor become despondent, but with great confidence submit ourselves to Your holy will, which is Love and Mercy itself.

—A prayer from *The Diary of Saint Maria Faustina Kowalska: Mercy in My Soul*

May 2021

COVID-19 lingers, but the number of cases is starting to drop in our state. Courts are reopened but are accessible only through zoom. (For an update on Drew's living situation, see chapter 100. Nothing except the year and the air temperature has changed.) The judge questioned him on how he was paying his cell phone bill since that seemed to be his only financial responsibility. He said that once in a while, a friend gave him a few dollars. Drew has become increasingly elusive without an address, and the judge ordered him to established one either through the postal system or by using a friend's address.

During the second court date, Drew was not held responsible

for not achieving an address; instead, he was given another extension and the suggestion that he contact a specific support program.

During the third court date, Drew admitted that he hadn't contacted the support program, and the judge converted his suggestion for Drew to enter the program into an order.

During the fourth court date, Drew wasn't penalized for not registering with the support program. Instead, he once again gained the judge's pity and was granted another extension despite the program offering job placement and emotional support.

During the fifth court date, the judge assigned a sixth court date in person.

During the sixth court date, Drew was handcuffed and sent to jail for nonpayment of child support. The judge set a seventh court date, which I asked to be excused from due to missing so much work for court. The judge granted my request verbally and in writing.

Drew posted bail within twenty-four hours of his arrest. A few weeks later when the seventh court date arrived, he did not appear, and a capias warrant was issued.

During the eighth court date, the capias was vacated and the contempt was concluded. When I researched why, their files showed that Drew had made a child support payment, and I was required to contact my case worker. When I contacted my case worker, he faulted me for not showing up for court to defend my case even though I had been excused from doing so. Because of that, I was unable to achieve any favor from my so-called supportive case worker. I filed a motion to reconsider.

During the ninth court date, the judge confirmed that even though I had been dismissed previously, my absence made my case weak, and Drew's previous bail amount was enough to count as a child support payment. The judge asked me for documentation to prove that Drew was capable of making future payments, which I had no way of providing. The motion was denied, and to date, the capias remains lifted.

It's been over a year since we have seen Drew for any kind of father-type visit. As far as we know, he remains homeless. Only randomly and seldom do we receive notification of his vitality.

Weeks after the last court date, I decided to call that same program that the judge had previously ordered Drew to contact. I was curious to see if they had offered any emotional support to the abandoned child or single mother. They did not. This prompted me to continue to research. I found only one credible program that offered mentoring for children, but it had an extensive waiting list—six to twelve months—and wasn't structured specifically for the fatherless. That was way too long of a wait for an emotional crisis.

I came across another program that supported the development of boys to some level, but again, it wasn't structured specifically to support the absence of a father, and girls weren't allowed in the program. Out of curiosity, I invested some time to see if there were any community programs to support fatherless girls. To date, I haven't found any. I continued to reach out in hopes of finding support for mothers of fatherless children, yet very little help was identified. After many nights with barely a nap for breaking in between, my exhaustion became almost unbearable as it was simultaneously being propped up by a strong desire for justice. Yet after a few dozen more attempts, I still wasn't able to realize any support specific to these matters.

I decided to compile this research with the research of fatherlessness I started shortly after Amie's death hoping to discover answers to the missing links. From this collaboration, the idea of raising awareness of the effects of fatherlessness and offering support to fatherless children and their caretakers was born.

CHAPTER 105

Never look down on anybody unless you're helping them up.

—Jesse Jackson

September 2021

We walked down the dusty broken road with the sun shining strongly on our faces, a path spread out before our steps towards the moment we've waited for years to enter. Countless shuffling feet poured out from huts with welcoming smiles and waving hands. Toby tossed handfuls of candies their way and they reached to catch the treats that were so rare to them and in that moment, Toby was the light of their world.

There was no doubt that we were very fortunate to be US citizens, however so many of us seemed to have lost sight on how to live life. Perhaps somewhere in our consciences we know we have access to become millionaires but the frustration, greed and pride it takes to accomplish this if approached carelessly costs our character to forfeit a level of compassion that separates us from humanity. I was glad to have taken that walk in Nigeria to realize life again. The treasure of satisfied joy that brought us thousands of miles from our home was so surreal, and it felt so good to be in that gift of time surrounded by love, far from the shadows of despair. It was indeed as much or perhaps more of a present to Toby and I as it was to the local community we had set out to help.

As we approached the opened gate, we saw the glorious queen of mercy standing strong and bold and ready. Upon her steps, villagers waited for our arrival and greeted us with songs of delightful thanksgiving. The king and queen arrived, the choir began to sing and at the head table, we sat to indulge in a feast of fish, goat, pumpkin leaves, egusi soup, fufu, rice and wine. Hundreds of people attended the ceremony together with fifteen priests, eight medical doctors, seventeen nurses, and twenty-one lay workers including myself and Toby. Toby had the best job of handing out reading glasses to all the people who needed them.

To our sides, children swarmed around with laughter as they jumped to hit colorful balloons that floated over their heads. We watched Fr Ebuka cut the ribbon at the front door entrance of the hospital and suddenly Toby and I noticed her in the crowd. She was wearing a beautiful red dress with a ruffled hem and belt along her waistline. Her face was wonderfully covered in faith and her name, Joy was defined by her luminous, grateful smile. As she stared back at us, she slowly lifted her hand and waved. I slowly lifted mine in return and Toby lifted his. In that moment, time healed all of the past time.

The music continued to play and a handsome doctor approached me. His eyes were soft and kind and his face was gentle when he asked, "May I have this dance with you?" And then we danced slowly in a moment that was surrounded by restored life until the sun resigned from the sky.

CHAPTER 106

When you reap your harvest in your field and forget
a sheaf in the field, you shall not go back to get it.
It shall be for the sojourner, the fatherless, and the
widow, that the Lord your God may bless you in all
the work of your hands. (Deuteronomy 24:19 ESV)

An inspiring rhetorical homily from Fr. Ebuka.

"In the book of the prophet Job, the first reading calls for deep
reflection. What we hear from Job, many have referred to it as the
dark night of the soul. It's often the result of adversity, or our attitude
in adversity. In this stage, one could feel alone and lonely, completely
vulnerable, full of sadness and sorrow. For some, that moment is
called despair. It is a tendency to capitulate, a kind of fatalism and
a belief that destruction is inescapable. There is almost a fascination
with one's doom. It happens to the best of us. Despair is a disease.
It is preying on one's self. It is like an obsession that something bad
is going to happen to oneself and that oneself is ruined. It is a very
sad place to be.

"Job was there in today's reading. He lost his health, his wealth,
and worst of all he lost his family. Life had little meaning for him.
What was there to live for? In despair, Job had to say to himself, *I
shall never see happiness again. Never*, he said. The view at the time

this particular book of Job was written was if we are good, things will go well for our lives, and if we are bad, all kind of terrible things will happen to us. But we know that that is not necessarily the case. There can be three reasons for adversity: we can bring it upon ourselves, others can bring it upon us, or it can be a test from God.

"In Job's case, it was a moment of test. So that's why we hear this message in the letter to the Hebrews 12:6 (NLT), 'For the Lord disciplines those he loves, and he punishes each one he accepts as his child.' The testing of faith leads to righteousness and to maturity in faith. A lot of times, God wants us to move from test to testimony—the testimony of His goodness. It could be caused by a loss, stress, betrayal, a diagnosis that seems disastrous, health challenges, loss of a job, accused of something you did not do, a cheating spouse—there are too many things to cause us to want to despair, things that begin to make us say that this is not fair. Indeed, life seems unfair sometimes, but we can treat ourselves in a fair way.

"Many of these situations are capable of bringing us plenty of tears, but there comes a time when we need to ask ourselves, is this worthy of tears? In the end, after all we heard in the first reading today, Job's story had a happy ending. It was because he came to the realization that God belongs to all, and all belongs to Him. It ended well because he was able to acknowledge the power of God when he said, 'I know that He lives.' And then he testified that the blessings of today and tomorrow shall be greater than those of yesterday. It was a statement and affirmation of the absolute power of God, but it was also a prayer.

"When he began to pray, he began to win. So through his challenges, he accepted himself into a prayerful way. He had a line of communication with God that was always opened. So Job's story has a happy ending, and our stories can also have happy endings. It's been said that even a caged bird can sing with joy. This bird can sing because it sees a future even in the cage. It sings because it sees beyond that cage. It sings because its spirit is not bound, it is not caged. It sings because it sees through the pitch darkness. The irony of life is that we must arrive in the darkest hour of night before morning arrives. And maybe it is in that pitch darkness that we can see the clearest.

"I know a story of two sisters who were twins. They were raped by their uncle, both of them. It was very devastating for them, so devastating that they actually contemplated suicide. Fortunately, they accepted to go for therapy. One made it okay. Years later, she went back to school, studied social work, and later opened an organization to assist victims of sexual abuse. Her twin sister on the other hand, despite going for therapy, became a drug addict and a sex addict and sadly died of a drug overdose.

"The same situation that makes the best out of one person can make a beast out of another. Life belongs to those who refuse to eat dust even after they have fallen. They rise like the phoenix from the ashes. Perhaps you have been there. Perhaps you have had these kinds of experiences. Me too. You are not looking at someone who has had a perfect life. I have been imperfect in so many ways. Growing up, I was very, very unhappy. I lived in the midst of a crowd, and yet I was unhappy. I watched other kids like me growing up with their fathers. I didn't have one. I didn't even have the chance of knowing what he looked like, how he could speak, how he could smile. I was too miserable at times—Christmas, Father's Day. I felt so lonely in those moments.

"To make matters worse, all my older siblings were away, and my younger one had an incurable illness that required my mother's constant attention. So I was raised in a boarding school, lonely in a crowd for a really long time. Until suddenly I was able to psycho-educate myself that I could not continue to live that way. How could I forget my life to misery? So I made a conscious decision that I was going to change the direction of my life.

"When I was in boarding school, every Sunday, parents would visit. Mothers and fathers would bring their children food and other items. During these times, I became extremely miserable because my mother couldn't travel and my father was dead. How could he come from the grave? I was so very miserable. So I began to feel like I could not stay in school. Sometimes, I would leave school for weeks and would not go back because it made me miserable to be there.

At one point, I left school and went to the city. I had some money that was meant for my books. I saw street gamblers. It felt enticing. I used that money to gamble. I thought I was going to win, but I lost my money. I was so sad that I lost, but God knew why I lost—He didn't want me to be a gambler. Maybe if I had won, the love of winning through gambling would have shaped me in a way that would have made me addicted to gambling. But God had other plans for me. At the time, I was only twelve years old.

And so because of my irresponsible behavior, I was thrown out of school. I ended up being dismissed from the seminary and went to a public school for three years. But during those years in this school, I vowed that I was going to rewrite my history. It became a moment of illumination for me. I started to think about all the good things I had heard about my father, how he had always cared for his family and looked out for the widows in our village.

"I was told that the night before he died, we went to northern Nigeria so he could find work, but he was discovered by terrorists. He had me with him, and somehow, he was able to find shelter for one night in a church, where he brought me with him behind the altar and slept there with me wrapped in his arms.

"The following morning, I was found alone by a nun and returned to my mother. Years later, I was told that a terrorist took my father's life on that last night he was sheltering me. At that time, I was barely fifteen months old. So I started to think about what his wish for me would have been. Why had he brought me there? He couldn't have given me a better gift. It was almost like he knew he couldn't escape his death, and so he went to hand me over to God.

"So as those thoughts come back to my mind, I knew I was dishonoring my father by destroying my life. And I wondered what he would have wished to see me become. So I started to study up. Within two years of being in this school, I was appointed the academic prefect of the school and became the role model for the rest of the students. I began to rise from grass to grace. You see, your attitude can determine your altitude; how high you can go. I was in this school for only three years, graduated high school at that time, and came out top of my class. I applied to go back to the seminary to continue my seminary training from the same place I had been thrown out of three years earlier. I was fifteen then. When I arrived, the same priest who had thrown me out, after looking at my grades, gladly embraced me and welcomed me back. I received a bachelor's degree in religious education, graduated summa cum laude; and bachelor's degree in theology, graduated summa cum laude.

"This was someone who was once completely lonely in the ruins of hopelessness.

"After my studies, I became an ordained priest. Within that same year, because of my excellent academic grades, I was sent to the Vatican to study. At the Vatican, I received a master's degree in theology graduating summa cum laude; a master's degree in philosophy graduating summa cum laude, and then a MBBS graduating summa cum laude. At the same time I was studying for my MBBS, I registered for a master's program in endocrinology, so one week after I defended my doctoral dissertation, I defended a master's dissertation in endocrinology. Currently, I am continuing my studies in psychology.

"You know, your destiny is in your hands. It depends on what you want to do with it; it is in your hands.

"So you see, somehow, God entrusts your future, your life, the whole of your being unto you. You cannot allow yourself to be ruined by adversity. There is too much at stake for you to do that. There is more about you than the challenges you face. Storms can come our way, but not every storm that comes your way is there to ruin your life; some are there to open doors wider for you.

"I couldn't think of a better way to honor my father than to turn my life around. I vowed, I was determined, and it happened.

"As I was writing my homily early this morning, around three, I looked over my shoulder at a photograph of my father hanging there and felt his pride for me. It was as if he were telling me, *Yes, you have done exactly what I would have loved for you to do, and you are exactly who I would love for you to be.*

"So he has remained my source of inspiration. And I'm glad I never wasted the opportunities I had in my life. We all can do the same, all of us.

"I did something else to honor him, which many of you know about. I started a nonprofit to help poor widows and orphans. As we speak today, I proudly sponsor eighty-eight widows, providing them with monthly grants for their feeding and medical care. Eighty-five orphans are in school today thanks to my efforts and the efforts of many, some who are here in church today. This all happened because I was inspired by my father's memory.

"So what is the reason I am saying all this? The loss of my father was my weakness, but thoughts of him became my strength. We can be strong where we are wounded. We can be strong from our wounds and injuries. God will always show up if we don't give up. Rock bottom can be a great foundation on which to build.

"In the beginning, my father was my only inspiration, but that has changed. You have all become my additional sources of inspiration—your encouragement, your kindness, your perseverance, your love.

"Now, I'm not telling this story just to boast. I'm telling in hope that I too can become a source of inspiration for you as you deal with your own trials. May God help us today no matter what we may be facing, no matter what challenges are in our way. Let us know that the Lord heals the brokenhearted, He is with us, and He never abandons us, amen."

—Rev. Fr. Ebuka

CHAPTER 107

Dear Optimist, Pessimist, and Realist. While you guys were busy arguing about the half-full or half-empty glass of water, I drank it.

—Sincerely, Opportunist

February 2022

So what's the distinction between widows and orphans and a woman with a child who has been abandoned by her husband? Other than the language and choice of free will, not much.

I was walking through a department store when I accidently bumped into a shelf causing a wooden sign to tip on its side. I picked it up. It read, "Only God can turn this mess into His messages." I grinned. It must have been meant for me. I bought it.

A few weeks later, I returned to that store for another copy of that sign. Although there had been several of them there when I saw the first one, there wasn't a single one to be found. *Okay, God. You know I came here to purchase that same sign for Fr. Ebuka. Can you please help me find it?* Several minutes later, still no sign. So I started walking toward the exit when appearing in plain sight on an end cap shelf all by itself was a wooden sign that read "God gave me you."

Once again, I grinned. *Thank you, God, for reminding me that Your plan is always better than mine.*

I bought that sign. I gave it to Fr. Ebuka and told him this story. While holding it, he smiled and said, "Yes, and God also gave me you."

Fr. Ebuka had been given a new assignment and will be relocating again, this time to a different state over three hundred miles away.

Many moments during these chapters of my life had been marked by the same month and even the same day but different years, and this was no different. My time with Fr Ebuka had made a complete circle and although my heart was heavy with grief, I couldn't have been more grateful for this incredibly humbling experience.

PART IX

EVOLUTION

The voyage will not teach you anything if you do not accord it the right to destroy you— a rule as old as the world itself. A voyage is like a shipwreck, and those whose boat has never sunk will never know anything about the sea. The rest is skating or tourism.

—Nicolas Bouvier, *Le Vide et le Plein*

CHAPTER 108

When people say to me, "I don't know how you went through all that and you're still standing," I have to give it some thought because I am standing and standing strong. Yet sometimes, people or perhaps certain personalities seem to be more comfortable when I find something to complain about. It's as if they expect that I should be forever damaged. There is no doubt that trauma needs to be validated and mourned, but then, it needs to be given a new identity so the previous memory loses its power to debilitate and new meaning is achieved.

The difficult part is not explaining when I have a sad moment, because sometimes I still do, but trying to explain how the whole of my life exists in a joyful, satisfied state of being. It took some time to figure out why my result was this way until I realized I had mentally organized my story from end to beginning, not beginning to end. I don't spend my time dwelling on the beginning of my adversities, which is the painful part. That could result only in keeping me in the mindset of a victim. Instead, I visualize my future as if it were already a part of a past with the intention of making everything that had happened have good meaning. It became a total eclipse over defeat, and the role I envision for my future self takes place almost naturally. Notice that I use the word *naturally*, not *easily*.

Devoid conscious evolution and life could settle into a state of addiction to cortisol, a chemical our bodies create in response to stress. We can get to a point that we automatically expect bad things to happen to us because we think we are doomed to constant bad luck and actually become uncomfortable when good things happens. From there, we may subconsciously do things to get back to the state of feeling stressed to receive another dose of cortisol.

Without applying good meaning, it's very difficult to enter the final stage of grief with a positive attitude, one of acceptance and hope. Now when I look back at those broken years, I wonder what happened to all the great stress that should have ruined me.

In addition to joy, I experience an abundance of freedom. Because I realize now that the saddest moments of my life weren't when I felt unloved by people who I thought were supposed to love me but when I found it difficult to love myself as a result. Although my predator is clearly unstable and lurks in the unknown, my peace lies in the freedom that exists in me and in the present moment not to be tarnished by a never-ending strand of what-ifs. Even if it all ended today, no one could take my peace, not even Drew, and that makes me much less a prisoner than he is.

No influence on earth can detach the dignity born from the death of our experiences once we insist on their meaning. For the purpose of finding hope for the fatherless, I suffered and died gracefully, not miserably. These thoughts are my God-given free will to choose.

CHAPTER 109

> Our success is judged by the way people view our life, but our spirit is judged by the level of our satisfaction.
>
> —Nora Greyson's journal

The Blossom

Today's date: Now and forever more.

I threw down a soft blanket over fresh green grass. He looked at me, and his freckles glistened as if God had pulled the shine from the sun and tossed it onto Toby's sweet face.

"There was a hole, in the center of the earth. It was a very big hole, just waiting for you. And in this hole was a very big star and this star was waiting for you. And in this star was a very bright light, and this light was waiting for you. And then one day, this very wise boy, he took this light and sprinkled it around. And around and around; and around and around; and around he went; for the whole world to see."

I embraced Toby. "Like the flu shot, you squeezed your eyes with the anticipation of a pinch only to realize it was over, and now you can appreciate the pain you just went through because it'll provide a better future. You've done it, Toby. You've built your time machine and changed history. This is the change I was talking about that is so beautiful. You see, all things really are possible with God."

"But it still hurts that Daddy doesn't see me."

"So let it hurt, and then let it go by thinking about how strong and how very important you are. I'm so proud of you for never having lost faith. You, my son, have made me realize that together we can really make a difference."

I rest on the blanket and look at the sky. God is my most fascinating and most favorite artist. Just look at this beautiful sky. "Imeela," I say—"I appreciate you" in Nigerian.

God is Love is God—The most beautiful complete circle.

At each bend, He was there just waiting my will. Today, I came down from the bleachers.

> These are the days that I've been missing. Give me the taste; give me the joy of summer wine. These are the days that bring new meaning. I feel the stillness of the sun, and I feel fine.

> These are the times of love and meaning. Ice of the heart has melted away and found the light. These are the days of endless dreaming. Troubles of life, floating away like a bird in flight.
>
> —Jamie Cullum

ACKNOWLEDGMENTS

I'm humbled and honored to have received the grace of God that allowed me to compose this token of my immortality. To the superior Artist who constantly creates and recreates all that is good and beautiful, thank You for Your interventions, Divine Mercy and for sending the Holy Spirit. Thank You for this beautiful life and Your endless compassion, faithfulness, patience, kindness, and love. Thank You for carefully carrying me through the fire and blessing me with great friendships, wisdom, prudence and strength along the way. You placed my feet on solid ground alongside the noble and the great even though I did nothing to deserve it. All glory and honor is forever Yours.

For the fatherless and victims of domestic violence, thank you for inspiring me to have the courage to publish this story. It was like untangling a twenty-year daily spinning knot to create a 200- page resume for a job position that has yet to exist, but if it helped in any way, it was worth it.

Many men struggle with being emotionally involved with their children even if they are physically and financially at their best. Results indicate that emotionally absent fathers are just as devastating to children's development as physically absent fathers. It is my deepest desire to raise awareness of fatherlessness, strengthen relationships between fathers and their children, support children in emotional crises who have no contact with their biological fathers, and provide them and their caretakers with compassion, empowerment, and dignity. So I thank everyone who has read this book. I hope in some way it was helpful. Please know that every review left on Amazon is appreciated and considered carefully by the author.

Thank you to my parents, extended family, and friends of whom there are so many. Mom, your instinctive devotion and irrefutable sacrifices never went unnoticed. Thanks for always caring. Dad, thanks for having my back with your fantastic left-brain skills, which I will never be able to wrap my head around, and for your handiness. Thank you both for always showing your dedication and to extended family for offering support.

Thank you to my church family and charitable committee for continuously proving that good people exist. While God may have guided your hands to open the door for me, it was through faith that I chose to show mercy to the most helpless people I've ever seen, and in return I received God's mercy through all of you. Each one of you had played a specific roll in His plan to demonstrate that the circle of divine mercy exists through faith. Because of this I found an incredible amount of hope and encouragement during a time that seemed like it should have been in complete despair. Thank you for being the testimony to what excellence and faith are all about.

Thank you to the two church girls who heard God's calling to lift my life. For your exceptional strength, loving intervention, constant prayers, and undeniable dedication, you will remain sacred in my heart.

Thank you to my closest childhood friend for your forever faithful friendship and sisterhood. You have always been my number one cheerleader, and I am grateful for your committed love and loyalty. It means the world to me.

Thank God for neighbors who display great wisdom, enduring support, and constant rescue. The world would be a better place if everyone could be as kind as you both have been.

Thank you to my sister in Christ for showing me the lifesaving virtue of self-control and most important for the constant reminders of God's incredible presence.

Thank you to my devoted priest for your examples of unshakable piety, leadership, compassion, patience, and kindness and for being the exceptional caregiver God called you to be, for inspiring me and for teaching me about moral gratuity. Thank you especially for never allowing me to get stuck in open wounds. If the bible were written today, there's no doubt you would be in it and identified as a saint. For all the lives you saved both physically and spirituality, no less of an honor would be appropriate.

Because I like to save the best for last, this one is for you, my dear son. Just look at how much more wonderful the world is because you're in it! I thank God for the gift of your life and for trusting me to guide you through it. Your light is your gift. It is a bright and beautiful gift that I believe God pulled from the heart of the sun and wove into your soul. Let the whole world see it, and never stop sprinkling it around. Never lose sight of your tremendous value.

"You are the light of the world. A city set on a hill cannot be hidden; nor does anyone light a lamp and put it under a basket, but on a lampstand, and it gives light to all who are in the house. Let your light shine before men in such a way that they may see your good deeds and moral excellence, and (recognize and honor and) glorify your Father who is in heaven." Matthew 5:14-16, Amplified Bible (AMP)

A special appreciation to the good role models, mentors, mothers, grandparents, and other family members who double as father figures by relentlessly going above and beyond but most of all in recognizing the dignity of fatherless children who strive to become their very best as they navigate this world with the strength of an army; fatherless. You are not statistics; you are my heroes. Thank you for your inspiration. May God protect you and grant you wisdom and fortitude. St. Jerome Emiliani, the patron saint of abandoned children, pray for us.

For the ones who have built me up and the ones who have torn me down, I thank you. It takes both sunshine and rain to bloom. Even if I could go back to a place in time when sunflowers grew taller than me, I wouldn't change a thing because I wouldn't be who I am now. When we are grateful and choose to live with good purpose, we are happy. It's impossible not to be.

ABOUT THE AUTHOR

Lucia St Monica's first novel "Only God Can Turn This Mess Into His Messages" leads us to recognize the early signs of domestic violence and it's connection to fatherlessness as she opens our eyes to reconsider how we respond to our time on earth. Her life experiences and research is currently leading her to outreach several statewide family support based programs in search for answers to the missing links in our system as she strives to bring dignity to fatherless children and long overdue support to their caretakers.

Lucia is passionate about exemplified inspiration, cultural diversity and raising awareness of family issues.

Printed in the United States
by Baker & Taylor Publisher Services